A Pattern of
Landownership
in Scotland

Scotland has the most concentrated pattern of private landownership in Europe, with the majority of Scotland's land held by a small number of landowners with large estates. Scotland also has a unique system of landownership, which is still classified in legal terms as feudal.

This book describes the present pattern of landownership in Scotland set against the background of the nine centuries during which feudal landownership has operated in Scotland. A more detailed description of one county, Aberdeenshire, is used throughout to illustrate the wider pattern and show the degree of continuity over the centuries in the numbers and sizes of large estates, their distribution within Scotland and the composition of their owners.

The author has a wide knowledge of both the history and present circumstances of rural Scotland and is well equipped to tackle this important subject. His direct experience of landownership includes membership of a woodland management partnership which owns 1250 acres (500 ha.) in the Eastern Highlands.

Landownership has always been the dominant influence in rural Scotland and this book will be of interest to the many people who wish to know more about the Scottish countryside.

Orkney

Shetland

Caithness

Sutherland

Ross &
Cromarty

Nairn Moray Banff

Inverness

Aberdeen

Kincardine

Angus

Perth

Fife

Argyll

Dumbarton

C K

Stirling

W

East
Lothian

Renfrew

Midlothian

Berwick

Lanark

Peebles

Bute

Selkirk

Ayr

Roxburgh

Dumfries

Kircudbright

Wigtown

C — Clackmannan

K — Kinross

W — West Lothian

The Counties of Scotland

A Pattern of Landownership in Scotland

With particular reference to Aberdeenshire

by
ROBIN FRASER CALLANDER

Haughend Publications

Published by
Haughend Publications,
Finzean, Aberdeenshire AB3 3PP Tel: 033-045-264

The publication of this book has been assisted by a grant
from the Twenty- Seven Foundation.

ISBN 0 907184.13.8

Printed by Nevisprint Limited, Fort William, Scotland

Contents

Dedicated to
John McEwen
in his 100th year

Acknowledgements

I have benefited from the research of many people in writing this book, most especially Dr Ian Adams, Dr John Gilbert, Dr Ian Grant, John McEwen, Dr Roger Millman and Dr Loretta Timperley, and I am very grateful to all of them. Several people commented on drafts of the book and I am particularly grateful to Professor John Hargreaves, Dr James Hunter and Dr David Stevenson. Responsibility for any errors that exist in the book is, of course, entirely mine. I have tried to ensure correctness of detail and interpretation, but this book is not intended as a scholarly work. My personal interest in understanding landownership in Scotland was frustrated by the lack of readily available information. This book presents some of the results of my investigations into this important subject in the hope that these will be of interest and assistance to others.

I am very grateful to Carolyn Cummins for typing up the final manuscript. My greatest debt in producing this book has been to Rita Kelly. She has helped at all stages from the initial survey of landowners to the final publication and, throughout it all, she has helped me to find the time to complete the task.

Robin Fraser Callander,
Finzean, June 1987.

Chapter 1

Landownership in Scotland

Landownership in Scotland is a property system that completely embraces the whole country: the land and inland water, the surrounding coastal waters and seabeds, all the airspace above these areas and also the ground below them, down to the centre of the earth.

The laws of this system form the basis of the relationship between Scotland's two fundamental components as a country — people and place. It is through this system that the control and use of Scotland's land and natural resources are determined. Landownership is therefore of great significance.

Scotland's system of landownership is different from that in the rest of Britain because it is defined by Scots Law. The Scottish system is also unique in the modern world because the method by which land is owned is still legally classified as feudal.[1] Feudal landownership became established in Scotland during the 11th century and has survived remarkably unaltered for nine centuries. (For comparison, England abolished its feudal system from 1290).

A Pattern of Landownership

The simplest measurement of landownership within Scotland's feudal system is to identify the areas of land belonging to different owners. These areas or landholdings form a pattern of landownership on Scotland's 19 million acres (7.87 m. ha.) of land and this is the pattern described in this book.

Scotland has a distinctive pattern of landownership, with the majority of the land held by a few large-scale private landowners. For example, 60% of Scotland's land area is owned by 1,430 landowners (Scotland's population is 5.1 million).[2] The pattern of large-scale landholdings or estates amongst these main landowners is itself dominated by fewer and larger estates: 50% of Scotland is held by 579 landowners, 40% by 269, 30% by 134, 20% by 49 and 10% by 13.

These statistics mean that Scotland has the most concentrated pattern of private landownership in Europe. 75% of all privately owned land in Scotland is held in estates of 1,000 acres (405 ha.) or more, 50% in estates of 5,000 acres (2,025 ha.) or more, and 33.3% in estates of 20,000 acres (8,097 ha.) or more. For comparison, even 100 years ago, when England was considered still dominated by large estates, less than 7% of England's land was held in estates of 20,000 acres or more.

A prominent feature of Scotland's estate structure has been the degree of continuity it has shown throughout its historical development since the arrival of feudal landownership. Precise figures are not available for the early part of this long history, but the trends are clear. During the first five centuries, up until the 17th century, the number of landowners increased. For example, in the 13th century, when the Crown and the Church owned many large estates, estimates suggest there were about 2,000 other landowners. By the early 17th century, when virtually all the former Crown and Church lands were in private ownership, the number of landowners was about 10,000. However, only 1,500 of these were major landowners.

In the 17th century, the trend of the earlier centuries reversed and the overall number of landowners started to decline. This new trend continued throughout the 18th century and into the early 19th century, by which time the number of landowners in Scotland was down to about 7,500. The fall was due to a reduction in the number of small landowners and the extent of Scotland held by the 1,500 largest estates showed a marked increase. These estates maintained their position during the 19th century and by the 1870s, for example, 90% of Scotland's land was still owned by less than 1,500 landowners.

During the last 100 years, the number of landowners has increased, but the underlying pattern of estates has remained fairly constant. For example, the change in the number of estates of 1,000 acres (405 ha.) or more between the 1870s and 1970s, was only a reduction from 1,758 to 1,723. The more signficant change was that the extent of Scotland held by these estates fell from 93% to 63%. This reduction is very largely accounted for by the growth of state owned land during this period from 0.2% to nearly 13% of Scotland and the increase in owner-occupied farms to cover approximately 11% of Scotland. The spread of urban land accounted for another 1.5% of Scotland's area beween the 1870s and 1970s, but had little effect on the overall estate structure. Over 97% of Scotland's total land area is still classified as rural land.

The composition of Scotland's estate owners shows, like the estate structure, a relatively high degree of continuity from past centuries. There have always been new entries to the ranks of Scotland's main landowners, from the Anglo-Normans who arrived with feudalism, to recent foreign buyers. However, since the Anglo-Normans, the different types of incomers during each century have never acquired more than a relatively small percentage of Scotland.

Thus, while all the phases of Scottish landownership are represented amongst the present estate owners, it is estimated that, for example, possibly 25% of all estates of 1,000 acres (405 ha.) or more have been held by the same families for 400 years or more. Amongst these owners are families that have been the hereditary occupiers of the same land for more than 30 generations since the arrival of feudalism and a particular predominance of families from around the 13th and 14th centuries. Over and above this 25% is a further significant percentage of today's estate owners who, while their families have held their present estates for less than 400 years, can trace their landowning ancestry for at least that length of time.

Both the extent of large estates in Scotland and the composition of their owners, owe more to events and trends many centuries ago than to any recent influences. As a result, some knowledge of the historical development of Scotland's pattern of landownership can make an important contribution to understanding the present pattern. An account of this historical background is provided in Part I (Chapters 2-6).

This historical development, while it reflects clear national trends, also shows marked differences between counties. For example, the counties that had the greatest concentration of large-scale private landownership in the 13th century, are typically still the counties with the most concentrated patterns of private landownership. The national pattern has to be understood at the level of the Scottish counties and within each county there are again variations between local districts. The description in Chapters 2-6 is therefore based on a detailed study of a single county set against the developing pattern in the other counties of Scotland. The fuller information for a single county provides additional insights into the wider pattern and also gives a clearer picture of the continuity over the centuries, by using examples from a single area. The names of landowners and their estates may be specific to that county, but the numbers of landowners and the sizes of their estates can be compared with elsewhere.

The county used is Aberdeenshire, one of Scotland's largest and most varied counties. Its 1.25 million acres (0.5m. ha.) straddle the important Highland:Lowland boundary and stretch from the peaks of Scotland's premier mountain range, the Cairngorms, across the largest tract of arable land in Scotland, to the Buchan coast. Aberdeenshire is not presented as being "typical", as no single county can ever represent the local variations within Scotland. However, the history of Aberdeenshire illustrates all the phases of feudal landownership in Scotland and, at those dates for which information is available for all Scotland's counties, the figures for Aberdeenshire have always been close to the national average.

During the long history of feudal landownership in Scotland, the whole surface of the countryside has never been divided into individual properties. Freshwater lochs, for example, remain up to the present day as a form of shared or common property, unless they are entirely enclosed within the estate of a single owner. Historically, a great extent of Scotland's land survived within the feudal system as shared or common land. Modern authorities state that, "It is our belief that very little, if any, common ground exists in Scotland".[3] The loss of common land in Scotland can be compared with the position in England. Estimates suggest that half the land areas of both Scotland and England were still common land in 1500. By the 1870s, 2.5 million acres (1 m. ha.) had survived in England and 1.25 million acres (0.5 m. ha.) of common land still exist there at the present time. Common land was already considered virtually extinct in Scotland by the 1870s and as early as 1828, the Lord Advocate had reported, "There is very little property in Scotland that is now common".[4]

Scotland had several types of common land, the most important of which were commonties. Their extent was greater than the combined area of all the other types of common land and their division is the main element in the disappearance of Scotland's common land. Scotland never experienced any Enclosure Acts equivalent to those that provided the mechanism for dividing common land in England. The Scottish Parliament passed a series of Acts in the 17th century to allow the division of commonties between neighbouring landowners. This legislation culminated in an Act of 1695 which provided a method for dividing commonties that was simple, quick and cheap, compared with the procedure in England. This single Act in Scotland enabled all commonties to be divided locally, while in England, the division of each area of common land required parliamentary permission. The

1695 Act survived the Union of Parliaments with England in 1707 and became the chief agent in the loss of Scotland's common lands. The 1695 Act still remains on the Statute books today.

The disappearance of millions of acres of common land into private ownership was a major episode in the development of the pattern of landownership in Scotland. Part 2 (Chapters 7-9) gives a history of Scotland's common lands, again using the example of Aberdeenshire to illustrate the wider Scottish story.

The Patterns Within the Pattern

The ownership of land in Scotland has always granted wide ranging rights over that land and these rights have conferred economic, social and political advantages on their holders.

Within Scotland's system of feudal landownership, the distribution of these rights of property or landownership does not coincide with the pattern of landholdings described in the following chapters. The owners in possession of land do not own their land outright and the purpose of this section is to place the pattern of landholdings within the wider context of Scotland's unique feudal system.

While the authority of all landowners in Scotland over their land has always been constrained by the general laws of the country, the rights of individual landowners over their land have additionally always been limited by the nature of their feudal title to that land.

Scotland's feudal landownership is a hierarchical system, within which all the rights of landownership derive from the highest authority in Scotland. In legal theory this is God, but in practice it is the Crown, who is the ultimate owner of all of Scotland. The Crown is known as the Paramount Superior and all other landowners are known as vassals of the Crown.

The essential feature of Scotland's feudal tenure is that the relationship between the Crown and its vassals need not be direct. Within this system, not only are certain rights reserved by the Crown but anyone, when they dispose of land they own in Scotland, can retain an interest in that land. They, as a vassal of the Crown, then become the superior of the new owner, who becomes their vassal. There is no limit in Scots Law to the number of times this process, known as subinfeudation, can be repeated over the same piece of ground. At each stage, superiors can limit the extent of possession conveyed by reserving rights to themselves and by imposing unlimited additional conditions and burdens on the vassals.

This system creates a hierarchy of interests in any piece of land, a feudal pyramid running down from the Paramount Superior at its apex, through subject-superiors, to the vassals at its base in actual possession of the land. These chains of superior-vassal relationships or tenure, and the different reservations and burdens at each stage, mean that the distribution of property rights in Scotland is dramatically more complex than the pattern of landholdings. This hierarchical system of relationships in Scotland's feudal landownership can be viewed as forming three distinct levels or types of pattern. This helps to simplify its archaic complexity and provide some context to the pattern of landholdings described in the following chapters.

The highest level is the interests of the Crown or "regalia". These principally consist of the sovereign rights that are considered to be held inalienably by the Crown (for example, the ownership of coastal waters) and other property rights which are reserved to the Crown, but capable of being granted out (for example, salmon fishings and the rights to minerals such as gold, silver, petroleum and natural gas).

The second level is the interests of superiority or "dominium directum", of which there may be several over any one piece of ground. The rights commonly reserved by superiors are those associated with minerals and sport, while the conditions imposed by superiors may often include, for example, a right of pre-emption and restrictions on the erection and uses of buildings.

The third level is the interests of the vassal in possession of the land. Known as the "dominium utile", these interests coincide with the pattern of landholdings. Below this level are tenants, who derive their rights of occupation and use from the vassal. The position of tenants is as old as the feudal system and, though the status of tenants has been traditionally contrasted with that of owners, the legislation governing tenancies has made tenants fully integrated components of Scotland's property system.

Amongst the three levels of ownership described, the interests of the vassals in possession of the land represent the least concentrated pattern of landownership. For example, estates that have sold off land and contracted to a small size, may have retained the mineral rights over the whole of their former estate. Thus the rights retained by superiors created "hidden maps" of landownership that are even more concentrated than the more conspicuous pattern of landholdings.

The relationship between superiors and vassals has altered little during the long history of feudal landownership in Scotland. In the earlier centuries, vassals mainly held their land in wardhold. This obliged them, amongst other conditions, to support their superiors with men at arms as often as was called for. In 1746, all wardholds from superiors were converted into feuholds which, again amongst other conditions, obliged the vassals to pay an annual fee or feu-duty to their superior.

Feuholds or feuing is still, with limited exceptions, the universal method by which land is owned in Scotland and the character of this relationship has changed little since the mid 18th century. Two of the most notable changes were in the 1970s. Firstly, in 1970, the superiors' perpetual right of pre-emption, which enabled superiors to buy back feus whenever they were going to be sold, was reduced to a once only option. Secondly, in 1974, the imposition of new feu-duties was prohibited and feu-holders were given the right to redeem any existing feu-duties or other perpetual ground rents by making a single larger payment to their superior.

In earlier centuries, feu-duties had been set as economic rents but, by the 1970s, most had become more or less nominal payments. Their removal, however, has not altered the feudal nature of land tenure in Scotland nor in any other way restricted the conditions and burdens that superiors can impose on their vassals within this system.

The authority of landowners over their land within Scotland's feudal system is therefore still limited, over and above the general laws of the country, by their feudal title to that land. The pattern of landholdings described in this book is both the simplest and the least concentrated pattern of landownership in Scotland.

Notes

1. There are several minor exceptions to this, principally allodial and udal tenures. Allodial tenure, which mainly involves lands held directly by the Crown and Church, is an integral component of the feudal system. Udal tenure, the remnants of which survive in the Northern Isles, is a more genuine exception to Scotland's feudalism.

2. The dateline for the most recent statistics on landownership in Scotland is 1970. The very limited changes since that time are discussed in Chapters 9 and 10. It should be noted that statistics for landownership in Scotland at different periods, frequently exclude the Shetland Isles and also often the Orkney Isles.

3. Scottish Rights of Way Society, 1979.

4. In Carter (1979).

Chapter 2

The First Five Centuries

The history of feudal landownership in Scotland has no precise beginning, as this system was only gradually introduced and not, in comparison to England, directly imposed by conquest.

Feudal landownership did not become fully established in Scotland for several centuries, but the death of Macbeth in 1057 was an important turning point. Macbeth was killed at Lumphanan in Aberdeenshire by his rivals for the Scottish Crown and was succeeded by Malcolm III, known as Malcolm Canmore. It was during the century between Malcolm's accession and the death of David I in 1153, the last of Malcolm's four sons to succeed him, that feudalism took firm root in Scotland.

Throughout the first five centuries of feudalism in Scotland, from the late 11th century to the end of the 16th century, land was the most powerful currency in Scotland. Feudalism was employed by Scottish kings as a well-tried system of law and order for strengthening their central authority and involved the promotion of power, based on the possession of land.

The Crown assumed ownership of all the land in the realm and then granted out authority over different parts of that land to others in exchange for financial and military obligations to the Crown. These owners could then grant out portions of their lands to others under similar conditions. This enabled the landowners holding direct from the Crown, often referred to as tenants-in-chief, to meet their commitments to the Crown. The granting out of land in this way, through several levels of landowners, established a pyramid of feudal authority with the Crown at its apex. The system aimed at control over all the lands of Scotland and, through decrees that everyone was required by law to have a lord, the whole population.

The introduction of feudalism into Scotland from the late 11th century was a product of Anglo-Norman influence. The feudal system itself had been developed in those areas and came later to Scotland. While feudalism was still developing in Scotland, it was already declining elsewhere and this was one of the main factors which resulted in Scottish feudalism having many of its own distinctive features. Another essential factor behind this distinctiveness was the degree to which the adoption of feudalism was based on adapting the existing system of land control in Scotland. Little is known about the arrangements that feudalism replaced, but it is clear that there was already a land based power structure and that the origins of this stretched back into prehistory, before Scotland itself emerged as a united country during the 9th century. (The Western Isles were not added to Scotland until 1266; the Northern Isles were annexed in 1612).

People had been living on the lands that were to be encompassed within Scotland for over 7,000 years before the arrival of feudalism. This history of settlement started with groups of hunter-gatherers and a territorial pattern of 'tribal' interests will have emerged at an early period. However, land itself only became a source of authority relatively late. It appears that up until about the 5th and 6th centuries A.D., the territorial pattern was still based on tributes levied by chiefs on the basis of kinship groups, rather than the occupation of land.

The progression of this arrangement into feudal landownership can be represented by the conversion of chiefdoms into lordships and of tributes into rent. Land was originally associated with kinship groups and chiefs derived their title in a reciprocal relationship with the group. Subsequently, the land became vested in the chief as the representative of the group. Finally, the land became the private property of the chief and the group's relationship to their land was only through their chief or lord. The chiefs' reciprocal relationship had become one with a higher authority beyond the group and this provided the authority or 'legal basis' of the chiefs' hold on the land. This was linked to changes in succession, so that the rights to the land became directly heritable through primogeniture, the whole estate passing to the eldest son. This was a change Macbeth's successors established for the line of succession to the Scottish throne.

The Scottish kings before Macbeth had already been increasing their central authority and administration. By the 11th century, a pattern of estates based on a territorial hierarchy was already established. After the king, the most powerful people were the Mormaers (literally 'high stewards'), who governed in the sub-regions of Scotland. Mormaers appear to have been the descendants of tribal kings and by the 11th century, when there were about 12 Mormaers in Scotland, they were both traditional chiefs and territorial magnates. Below these great Celtic nobles were the Toiseach (literally 'the first'), local leaders who had become increasingly identified as thanes by the 11th century. Thanages provided the basic pattern of estates, within which there were 'tenants' or 'free men'. Below the tenants were several forms of subtenants, making up the local population working the land. The Church also held land in the 11th century, which was held "free from Mormaer or Toiseach".

Scotland was a united though still very heterogeneous country by the 11th century and the pattern of thanages or early estates, reflected this in the variety of their size and character. Although records of them are mainly for the Lowlands and eastern Highlands, they also occurred in the western Highlands. 'Thane' literally meant 'to serve' and thanes were royal officers responsible for different districts. These districts correlated in most of Scotland with shires, with the larger shires having more than one family of thanely rank. From the thanes came the sheriffs, literally the shire officer or steward. The shires of the thanes were smaller than the pattern of counties and sheriffdoms established under feudalism between 1124 and 1286. However, the feudal pattern of counties was based on the original thanages and some of the old shires or thanages survived, such as Kinross and Clackmannan. Scotland's counties at the present time have thus existed throughout the period of feudal landownership in Scotland, though local government re-organisation in 1975 has now reduced their administrative significance.

The introduction of feudalism from the late 11th century was a development of the existing system of land control and the spread of feudalism proceeded on the pragmatic basis of what was possible, a balance between power and opposition. The concept of superiority eased the spread of feudalism because it did not directly change the existing pattern of landholdings. Feudalism represented a sharper definition of property rights, with these rights attached to specific areas of land rather than to individuals. The existing landholders had their own interests in strong lordship and the advantages of feudal authority were underpinned by the establishment of hereditary succession to the possession of land. This was the new right that created personal property in land and made private landowners out of traditional leaders.

Scottish kings during the early period of feudalism in Scotland had usually had direct experience of this system from living as feudal lords in England before coming to the Scottish Crown. The kings also imported Anglo-Normans to assist them establish feudalism and other Anglo-Normans arrived in Scotland because of the good prospects of obtaining land and gaining the power that went with landownership. Social status, political influence and economic opportunity all depended upon it.

The relationship of these kings with England was very important in promoting feudalism within Scotland. Malcolm Canmore, who succeeded Macbeth, had been educated in England and only managed to depose Macbeth and defeat Macbeth's traditional successor with English help. Malcolm married into the English royal family around 1070 and when he died in 1093, the succession was again disputed and only secured for his sons through the help of his widow's English relations.

At the time of Malcolm's death, the feudal and pre-feudal influences in Scotland appear to have been closely matched. By 1124, when David I came to the throne, Scotland could not yet be described as a feudal country. However, the king's position had been re-modelled in the Anglo-Norman style and all the first elements of feudalism established. Feudal control was then greatly extended by David I during his 29 year reign.

David I was already about 40 years old when he became king. He had lived for many years in England, where he had the earldoms of Northampton and Huntingdon with lands in eleven English counties. Many of the Anglo-Norman families whom David I brought into Scotland as part of his very active promotion of feudalism, came from these lands. These families were mainly granted lands in the Borders and the south of Scotland, though many of these families subsequently obtained greater lands elsewhere in Scotland. For example, many Anglo-Norman families who became major landowners in Aberdeenshire from the 13th century onwards started in the Borders during the 12th century, including the Bissets, the Comyns and, as immediate neighbours in Berwickshire, the Burnetts and the Gordons.

The conversion of native lords into feudal landowners during the reign of David I is illustrated by the two Mormaers with extensive territories in Aberdeenshire. The Mormaers of Mar (the Lord of the Hills) and of Buchan (the Lord of the Valleys) both adopted feudal titles at this time and became the Earls of Mar and Buchan. Similarly, most of the early sheriffs north of the Clyde-Forth line had Celtic names and must have involved traditional native landholders.

Landownership in Scotland

The basic feudal relationships between the Crown and its tenants-in-chief and between these great lords and their vassals had been established by Alexander I (1107-24). It was a form of knights' service, known as 'wardhold'. This derived its name from the right of superiors to the guardianship of their vassals and vassals' estates, if the vassals inherited them when under age or in 'minority'. The basis of this feudal tenure was the military obligation of the vassal to serve the superior in arms as often as required. There were also a wide range of other dues and duties that vassals owed to their superiors and to which they were, in turn, entitled to from any vassals of their own. These included 'aid' to ransom the superior out of imprisonment and 'relief' payable to the superior on the succession of an heir to the vassal. A breach of any of the host of these conditions and casualties by vassals could result in the forfeiture of their lands back to the superior.

The power of forfeiture was the basic weapon of the king and other feudal superiors, allowing them to re-distribute land amongst their loyal supporters. The lands held by Anglo-Norman families continued to expand by these means during the 12th and 13th centuries. Strategic marriages were also important and, for example, by 1284 four of the Celtic earldoms had passed to them through heiresses. The first was the earldom of Buchan in Aberdeenshire, to the Comyns in 1214. From the reign of David I, there had also been a major increase in the number of burghs, to expand and regulate trade and to increase the revenues of the Crown and other major landowners. During the 12th century, the pattern of parishes became established in Scotland and David I also promoted the expansion in lands held by the Church. By the late 13th century, the Church had acquired much of the best land in Scotland and had consolidated its own political and financial power.

By the end of the 13th century, although Scotland was still linguistically and ethnically mixed, there was a homogeneity of government and feudal control. Centralised royal authority from Edinburgh was pre-eminent and undisputed heriditary succession to feudal lands widely obeyed, even if the more outlying parts of Scotland could still be a law unto themselves. Feudalism had been established, with subsequent developments representing the consolidation of its coverage and control.

Considerable changes had occurred in the pattern of landownership and the composition of landowners with the rise of feudalism and its supporters from the 11th to 13th centuries. By the 13th century, the ownership of land was completely dominated by the Crown, the Church and a small number of great landowners or magnates. The balance between these interests varied from county to county, though the overall pattern still clearly reflected the pattern of control that had existed under the Mormaers and other powerful provincial lordships in the 11th century.

Details of the overall pattern of landownership in Scotland at this time, and up to the 16th century, are only beginning to be uncovered by researchers. The rest of this Chapter provides an outline of the evolution of the pattern during these centuries, as background to the more detailed description that is possible from the 17th century. Throughout the first five centuries of feudalism, there was a very close relationship between the history of feudal landownership and Scotland's history. Central to this was Scotland's troubled relationship with England and the need to repel the feudal threats posed by English claims to the Crown of Scotland and the superiority of all Scotland's lands.

The sketch map Fig 2.1 shows the pattern of landownership for Aberdeenshire in the 13th century. The two greatest landowners, the former Mormaers, the Earls of Mar and Buchan, controlled over half the county with the lands of the other landowners sandwiched between their large territories. The Crown and the Church held about 20% of the county. Crown lands were most prominent further south in Scotland in the triangle between Edinburgh, Stirling and Perth. The Church, through the Bishops of Aberdeen, had held land in Aberdeenshire since the early 12th century, and though a major landowner in Aberdeenshire by the 13th century, the county had no great monastic estates like those in many other counties.

The other landowners in Aberdeenshire in the 13th century reflected the wider mix between native and Anglo-Norman interests. The lands of Strathbogie were part of the earldom of Atholl which, like Mar and Buchan, descended from a Celtic Mormaer. The lands of Garioch had been originally established by William the Lion (1165-1214) for his brother David, the Earl of Huntingdon, whose descendants still held it during the 13th century. The Durwards were an Anglo-Norman family who, although not titled, had royal connections. The Durwards took their name from their position of hereditary door-keepers or bodyguards to the king. They were one of the most influential families in 13th century Scotland and aspired to the Scottish throne through a marriage to an illegitimate daughter of Alexander II (1214-49). This was unsuccessful, as was a claim in the mid 13th century to the title of Earl of Mar through their mother. However, the king, perhaps wishing to weaken this powerful earldom, did grant the Durwards extensive tracts of its Aberdeenshire lands in mid and lower Deeside. The

Fig 2.1   Sketch Map of Landownership
in Aberdeenshire during the 13th century

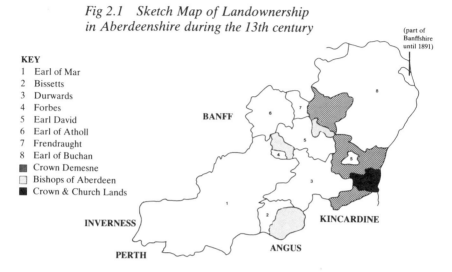

(part of
Banffshire
until 1891)

KEY
1   Earl of Mar
2   Bissetts
3   Durwards
4   Forbes
5   Earl David
6   Earl of Atholl
7   Frendraught
8   Earl of Buchan
■   Crown Demesne
☐   Bishops of Aberdeen
■   Crown & Church Lands

BANFF

INVERNESS

PERTH

ANGUS

KINCARDINE

Bissets, another Anglo-Norman family, also benefited from the reduction of Mar and obtained the lands of Aboyne and Glen Tanar in 1242. The other two landowners in the 13th century pattern in Aberdeenshire were native landowners who had held their lands since at least the 12th century (the Forbes and Frendraughts). The Forbes of Forbes parish claimed to be descended from the first family to settle their lands.

The Crown lands in Aberdeenshire during the 13th century are listed as demesne, as they were lands retained by the Crown rather than granted out. Demesne was of two types, general demesne, which covered the Crown's overall position as lord of any pieces of land not held by another through a grant, and specific demesne, the lands from which the Crown derived direct revenues and services. The sketch map Fig 2.1 makes the pattern of landownership appear very neat and orderly. However, ownership in the 13th century was more akin to an area of jurisdiction, where law and order were the responsibility of the landowners within the wider, central authority of the Crown. Landownership was not defined by tidy lines on a map.

A major part of the lands held directly by the Crown were designated as hunting forests and were governed by a comprehensive system of forest laws. Some of these forests were held for strategic reasons, but many were used by the kings for sport. Hunting was greatly valued in medieval Scotland and it appears that landowners probably spent more time, effort and thought on hunting than on any other activity. Fig 2.2 shows the wide distribution of forest hunting

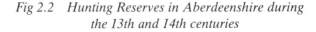

*Fig 2.2   Hunting Reserves in Aberdeenshire during
the 13th and 14th centuries*

KEY
☐   Hunting Reserves in the 13th century
○   Hunting Reserves first recorded after 1286
A   Culblean
B   Mar (Cambuskist)
C   Birse
D   Trostach
E   Drum
F   Cullerlie
G   Corgarff
H   Glencarvie
I   Invernochty
J   Mar (Kildrummy)
K   Leslie
L   Bennachie
M   Mar (Garioch)
N   Fetternear
O   Kintore
P   Kinmuck
Q   Fintray
R   Cordyce
S   Aberdeen
T   Tarves
U   Buchan

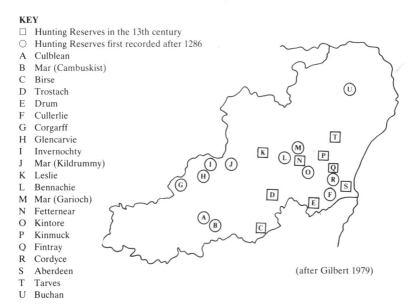

(after Gilbert 1979)

reserves in Aberdeenshire during this period, when there were more than 150 such forests in Scotland as a whole.

In the 13th century, the extent of royal demesne had steadily declined, but this had been a gradual process compared with the severe depletion that occurred in the 14th century. The initial cause of this at the beginning of the century was the Wars of Independence against England. The period had a dramatic effect on the pattern of landownership and composition of landowners. The lands of owners who had served on the losing side were forfeited to the Crown and then granted out as rewards to loyal supporters, which was also the fate of much Crown land. The changing fortunes of the wars and the volatile loyalties of some important families only served to increase the exchanges of land taking place. Robert Bruce made extensive use of land grants, his own ancestors being Anglo-Normans who had received land in Scotland from David I.

The fate of Aberdeenshire's two great earldoms, Mar and Buchan, were very different during this period. The Earl of Mar did not take a prominent part in the action. The 8th Earl had succeeded to the title in 1297 and died in 1305. The 9th Earl was then still a child and was held prisoner by the English until after Bannockburn. The lands of Mar

23

were, however, loyal to Bruce and remained unreduced by the wars as Bruce was the child Earl's uncle. The 8th Earl and Bruce had married each other's sisters and Bruce had given the 8th Earl the lordship of Garioch, which had reverted to the Crown. By comparison, the Comyn Earls of Buchan were prominent and bitter enemies of Bruce. In 1308 Bruce set out to destroy the Comyns and defeated the Earl of Buchan's forces at Barra, in the Aberdeenshire parish of Bourtie. All the Earl's lands were forfeited and broken up through grants and the name of Comyn was even proscribed for a time.

The collapse of a major family could affect the fortunes of many other landowners and the Comyns were one of the most powerful groups in Scotland at the time of their defeat, with John Comyn, the Earl of Buchan, the Lord High Constable of Scotland. The forfeiture of this title provides an example of two important families gaining their first footholds in Aberdeenshire. After the defeat of the Earl of Buchan, Bruce granted the title to the Earl of Atholl, but this title and the Atholl lands were also forfeited in 1319. Bruce then granted the title, together with much of the former Comyn lands in Aberdeenshire, to Sir Gilbert Hay, and he granted the Atholl lands of Strathbogie to Sir Adam Gordon. Both these knights had been valuable supporters to Bruce. Hay had been loyal to him throughout the strife, while Gordon had transferred to serve the English after Wallace's capture in 1305, only rejoining the Scots in 1313 in time to fight heroically at Bannockburn. The Hays subsequently became the Earls of Errol and the Gordons, amongst other titles, the Earls of Huntly.

The Crown had lost most of its own lands to Scotland's leading landowning families by the end of the 14th century, but the longstanding pattern of earldoms and provincial lordships had survived. By the 1320s, the twenty-nine of these that still existed had become concentrated under thirteen earls and five provincial lords, with the Crown still holding three. The Randolph, Stewart and Douglas families also held several each. However, the power of individual families was even greater by the 1390s. Two new earldoms had been created, but the thirty-one earldoms and provincial lordships were held by only fifteen magnates from ten different families. The Stewarts, Douglases and Dunbars holding twenty-two between them.

This overall longstanding pattern only really started to disappear in the 15th century. By the 1460s, only five of the old style earldoms survived, incorporating another five of the old lordships. These were held by the Earls of Angus, Atholl, Huntly, Ross and Sutherland. The Earls of Huntly had only been elevated in 1445, but held the ancient lordship of Strathbogie. Their new earldom was one of an increasing number of earldoms created as personal honours unrelated to the old style earldoms. Many of the old titles with their lands also returned to the Crown under James I (1406-37) and James II (1437-60) by forfeiture or eschaet and were not granted out again in the same fashion as before.

The reduction of the traditional pattern of territories associated with the earldoms and provincial lordships paralleled the fate of the holders of these titles. There had been 13 families of earls in 1300 and another 43 creations before 1469, yet by that time there were only 19 families of earls, mostly recent creations. There had been a consistent failure amongst the higher nobles to maintain direct father-to-son succession, with on average a quarter of the families failing in the direct male line every 25 year generation.

There was far greater consistency amongst the ranks of the landowners below the higher nobles. In 1300, there had been a total of 1500 or more landowners, but most of these were relatively small local lairds and there were only about 50 families that were important in national affairs. Around half these families were the higher nobility associated with the old earldoms and provincial lordships. The other half were the lesser nobility and there had been little change in the composition of these families by the mid 15th century. For example, five of these long-established families, the Hays, Keiths, Grahams, Setons and Somervilles had been important since the 12th century, more than twelve since the time of Robert I and three, the Douglases, Erskines and Lyons since the mid 14th century.

During the upheavals between the late 13th and mid 15th centuries, the old nobility largely disappeared and these longstanding families were left as the major landowners in Scotland. There were fewer changes in the pattern of landownership in the 150 years after 1450 than before it and these families maintained their dominance for centuries to come. The prominence of different families varied from county to county. In Aberdeenshire, the main families included the Burnetts, Farquharsons, Forbes, Frasers, Gordons, Hays, Innes, Keiths, Leiths, Leslies, and Ogilvies. Half of these families owed their first land grants in the county to Robert Bruce, while half dated from the 13th century or earlier. Many owned land outside Aberdeenshire and in several cases, the main family line was in another county. The Leslies, for example, were a cadet branch of the Earl of Rothes' family and the Ogilvies, subsequently the Earls of Findlater and Deskford, had their main seat in Banffshire.

Several families in the Aberdeenshire list received their earldoms in the mid 15th century. The Gordons became the Earls of Huntly in 1445, the Hays, the Earls of Errol in 1452 and the Keiths became the Earls Marischal in 1457. The first Earl of Huntly was Alexander Seton who had married the Gordon heiress in 1408. The title 'Huntly' derived from the first lands in Berwickshire that the Gordons had originally received in the 12th century. By the mid 15th century, the Earl of Huntly still owned these lands, together with their main lands in Aberdeenshire and other lands in Banff, Moray and Inverness-shire. The authority of the Earls of Huntly in the North-east reflected how the regionalised power structure which had existed since pre-feudal times still continued through the 15th century, even if the pattern and character of that power had been modified.

By the mid 15th century, the decline in the military significance of feudalism made the social alliances and political allegiances of land-owners increasingly important. The traditional feudal commitments between superiors and vassals became re-inforced by kinship ties and formal bonds of friendship or 'manrent'. Scottish kinship was agnatic, a bond between male relatives, and this made kin-groups readily identifiable through surnames. The alliances of kin were extended by the bonds of manrent in which landowners promised to support each other with men and money when either needed it. These bonds were typically between lesser and greater landowners who otherwise had no feudal connection or kinship ties with each other. They served to protect the lesser landowner and strengthen the power of the greater landowner. However, these bonds were also signed between leading landowners as, for example, between the Earls of Huntly and Errol in 1546, when they were the two most powerful landowners in Aberdeen-shire.

The emergence of these bonds in the mid 15th century was in part a response to the vacuum left by the disappearance of the old earldoms and provincial lordships. In Aberdeenshire, the loss of the Earldom of Mar to the Crown in 1435 and the re-granting out of parts of the Mar lands, produced a new situation in which these alliances were an important element. The three loyalties of feudal obligations, kinship ties and bonds of manrent all tended to stabilise local power structures and overall had a great influence in maintaining the pattern of landownership in the 15th and 16th centuries. Landowners widened their alliances to secure and strengthen their hold on their land and the power it conferred.

These three loyalties could produce a confusion of interests for individual landowners. Traditionally, there had been little distinction between feudal and family interests but, by the 15th century, as the pattern of landownership became more complex, there was a greater chance that these loyalties might not coincide. The conflict of loyalties between supporting a feudal superior or a branch of the family was a decision between land or blood and each case had to be weighed on its own merits. Bonds of manrent added an extra dimension to this situation, but they were the weakest obligation and the most easy to renege.

The position of the Forbes over the Douglas issue, which dominated events in Scotland for a decade in the mid 15th century, illustrates how these bonds could become a problem. The Forbes' superior had successively changed from the Earls of Mar to the Crown and then to the Earls of Huntly. Huntly, with whom the Forbes had quarrelled, supported the Crown against the Earl of Douglas, with whom Lord Forbes had signed a bond. The Forbes at this time had just acquired, through the 1st Lord Forbes, most of the lands that the family was to hold during the subsequent height of Forbes prosperity. These included the lands of Alford and Castle Forbes in 1423 and Corsindae in 1444. In the end, Lord Forbes decided that the longterm security of these lands was more important than the Douglas cause and begged leave of his bond. The eventual victory of the Crown and the subsequent royal favour towards the Forbes validated this decision.

Although kinship was based on agnatic linkage, marriages played an important part in the pattern of landownership. Strategic marriages added to direct kinship ties and were a prominent feature of the feudalism modified by kinship that was so characteristic of landownership in Scotland during these centuries. Marriages could be used to create or confirm alliances between families, to settle the succession to lands or to obtain the inheritance of lands. These strategic considerations tended to be the foremost factors in marriages. The prevalence of individuals being married more than once and the promiscuous relationships outside marriage, which could lead to illegitimate children subsequently disputing claims, all added to the complex web of relations between landowning families.

The importance of marriage was reflected in Alexander Seton's acquiring the Gordon estates in 1408. Marriage also played an important part in the succession of two of Aberdeenshire's oldest estates, dating from the 13th century. The Frendraught family had forfeited their Forgue lands to the Stewarts in the early 14th century. The lands then passed by marriage to the Frasers in 1442 and then through marriage again to the Morays and finally to the Crichtons, with whom the lands remained for several centuries. Similarly, the Bisset lands in Deeside had passed by marriage to the Frasers by the mid 14th century. Then, again through the female line, they passed to the Keiths and, by 1437, to the Gordons. In this latter instance, the Keiths complained they had lost too much land through the marriage and managed to negotiate an amicable settlement, which resulted in some of the lands being returned to them.

The changes in landownership through marriage most often benefited the more powerful families. The upward marriage of daughters, sent in allegiance into the household of the feudal superior or other greater landowner, was more common than for sons. This could result in the family's land passing to a younger son of that greater landowner and a cadet branch extending the estates of an already important landowning family. The traditional main landowning families were not only successful at maintaining their own direct male succession, but also produced many sons. Many of these sons became landowners of other estates and during these centuries the leading families established a large number of cadet branches. The two most prolific families in this respect in Aberdeenshire were the Forbes and Gordons. The 14th century head of the Forbes, Sir John the Black Lip, had four legitimate sons. Fifty landowning lines of Forbes arose from these sons over the next two centuries, a rate only exceeded in the county by the Gordons.

The continuing conflicts both locally and nationally could have a sudden impact on the fortunes of individual families in the 15th and 16th centuries. For example, the 3rd Baron of Balquhain, Sir Andrew Leslie, and his second wife, Isobel Mortimer, lost six sons in one day at the Battle of Harlaw in 1411. This type of loss was not infrequent when fighting was done in kin-groups. The dangers of conflicts were also reflected in the construction or substantial reconstruction of over 30 castles in the North-east during the 15th century. A wider impact on the landowning classes in Scotland resulted from the battle of Flodden in 1513 when the King, three bishops, 11 earls, 15 lords, and many other important landowners were killed. However, such national calamities were comparatively rare in Scotland during the century and a half from the mid 15th century. Similarly, both conflicts between the Crown and most powerful landowners and more local feuds were relatively limited.

During this period, the number of landowners in Scotland was increasing. For example, the lands of the earldom of Mar which had reverted to the Crown in 1435, were shared by 150 landowners by 1600. These new estates were nearly all either outlying portions of existing landowners' estates or else held by cadet branches of the main landowning families. This general increase was also reflected in the growth of baronies, estates held direct from the Crown and within which the landowner had jurisdiction through a barony court over theft, assault and accidental homicide. Their number had risen from around 350 in Scotland during the late 14th century, to over 1,000 by the end of the 16th century. Many important landowners held more than one barony, with the powerful Earls of Huntly controlling 11. The dispersed nature of the Huntlys' baronies in six counties reflected the increasing complexity of the pattern of landownership by the 15th and 16th centuries.

The greatest increase in landowners during these centuries came from feuing. This tenurial arrangement was an alternative to wardholding and replaced military obligations with payments to the superior. Feu-holding had taken place since the 12th century, but was still relatively uncommon by the 15th century. However, during that century, feuing became increasingly widespread, particularly on Crown and Church lands, with extensive feuing of Church lands in the 16th century. Many feus were granted to existing landowners, but it is estimated that around half went to new landowners. On Church lands in particular, these new owners were more likely to be the former tenants.

The Church had traditionally managed its estates without vassals, but had often had arrangements with neighbouring landowners. The Bishops of Aberdeen still had important lands in Aberdeenshire into the 16th century and since at least the early 15th century, had appointed hereditary baillies to safeguard their estates. The baillies were normally powerful landowners in their own right and more than once used their authority to exploit the Church lands under their protection. In 1489, Bishop Elphinstone had to take the hereditary baillie of the Bishop's Birse lands to court for illegally extracting stock and rent from the tenants. Subsequently, the Bishops appointed local baillies from the inhabitants on their Birse lands, but by then the office of Bishop, not just the Church's lands, was under the influence of the Earls of Huntly. The Earls became the guardians of the Bishops of Aberdeen and used their position to appoint Church officers from their own kin. For example, the 3rd Earl had his 4th son, William, installed as Bishop in 1546. This Bishop William Gordon was a conspicuous example of the type of prelate that brought the Roman Catholic Church into disrepute before the Reformation of 1560.

Bishop Gordon's disposal of the Church lands is illustrated by the lands of Birse, which the Bishops had held since the 12th century. In

1549, three years after becoming Bishop, he granted his first feu charter for lands in Birse. This charter was to his own elder brother, Sir Alexander Gordon of Strathaven, the 3rd son of the 3rd Earl of Huntly. The Bishop disposed of all the lands in Birse during the next ten years, 18 out of the 24 towns and the extensive Forest of Birse all ending up with Gordons. The position was much the same over the rest of the Bishop's Aberdeenshire lands, which had also included valuable salmon fishings, though not all the lands were lost willingly. In 1544, James Forbes of Corsindae had forcibly acquired a title to the church lands of Montgarry. He robbed Bishop Gordon's predecessor of the bulk of the church's treasures when they were being moved for fear of another English invasion. James Forbes then held the treasures for ransom until he received a charter for the lands. James' brother also obtained church lands but by less forcible means when he took over the Priory of Monymusk in 1549.

The Church had still been the wealthiest landowner in Scotland at the beginning of the 16th century, but before the end of the century it had lost virtually all its lands. Much had gone before the Reformation, particularly through feuing from 1530, as a response to increased taxation. In 1587, the final disposal of the Church's remaining estates started after the king had annexed these lands and begun granting them out to secular landowners. By the end of the century, both the Crown and the Church were reduced to relatively minor landowners. The Crown still held some important estates, for example in Fife and Strathearn. However, the original feudal pattern of landownership dominated by Crown, Church and nobles had disappeared. Instead, the pattern was completely dominated by private landowners, amongst whom the largest still came from the same small number of families that had been advancing their position since the 13th century. No accurate figures exist for landownership at this time, but in Aberdeenshire there were around 500 landowners of whom more than two thirds belonged to the twelve main traditional landowning families. Amongst these, the top 50 landowners held more than two thirds of the county. In Scotland as a whole, estimates suggest there were around 10,000 landowners, the great majority of whom were small local landowners. The pattern of landownership was dominated by less than 1,500 larger landowners.

The increase in the numbers of landowners during the 15th and 16th centuries had had little effect on the overall pattern of landownership amongst these main families. The increase had principally resulted from the granting of feus which had expanded the base of the feudal pyramid with many small landowners. Feuing had been very profitable for superiors. They obtained a substantial initial cash payment, followed by a fixed annual payment intended as a rent. This provided superiors with money, cattle and other goods with which to maintain or enhance their position. While the grantee did have security of possession, the land still remained controlled by the superior. The grant was heritable but only subject to the superior's approval and another cash payment for renewal of the feu charter. The superior could still resume possession or reassign the lands when a feu came up for renewal, making these feus more equivalent to tenancies as they are now perceived.

The spread of feuing was widely resented in the 16th century, as many tenants were displaced who could not afford to convert their tenancies into feus. Feuing was a part of the growth of land as a commodity from the 15th century, with wealthy burgesses from the burgh merchant communities increasingly active in the land market. The status of land as a financial commodity was also reflected in the late 16th century legislation concerned with land titles, which was designed to protect the financial investment that land had come to represent. In the second half of the 16th century, the value of feuing to superiors became increasingly focussed on the payments for obtaining the feu or renewing it. The annual payments were fixed and inflation during this period rapidly eroded their value. For example, the silver value of coins, which had fallen by half between 1513-1570, fell by half again before 1600. This switched the economic advantage more towards existing feuars and was to have important consequences for the pattern of landownership during the 17th century.

The spread and development of feudalism during its first five centuries in Scotland resulted in a pattern of landownership dominated by a small number of landowners whose families had built up their estates over the centuries. The progress of feudalism incorporated variations in different parts of the country, notably the Highlands. The slower penetration of feudalism into the Highlands reflected the weaker influence of royal authority there. However, the forfeiture of the Lordship of the Isles in 1493 had been an important step in bringing the Highlands within the central authority of the Crown. A century later, the Crown's control in the Highlands could still be tenuous but nearly every Highland chief had learnt the value of possessing feudal charters to their lands. A decree by James IV in 1597 requiring all Highland landowners to produce their titles was never fully implemented. However, by then all of Scotland had at last become covered by feudal tenure. Highland landowners were as

31

interested as landowners elsewhere in Scotland in maintaining and increasing the power they derived from their lands. Feudalism and Gaelic culture may have had many opposing elements, but the conversion of tributes into rents was a transition that required no significant changes in existing structures.

By the end of the 16th century, the end of the first five centuries of feudalism in Scotland, there was already a persistent pattern of estates held by the same families that had owned them for centuries. The number of landowners had increased markedly, but many only had a limited hold on their land. In the first half of the 17th century, when detailed records start to become available for the patterns of land-ownership in Scotland's counties, the total number of landowners started to decline. However, the traditional landowning families and their pattern of estates were to persist through the 17th and later centuries. The power that derived from landownership continued to enable those who held the land to maintain and strengthen their control over it.

Chapter 3

The 17th Century

The power associated with landownership throughout the 17th century meant that landowners continued to dominate economic, social and political life in Scotland, as they had done during the previous centuries. However, the 17th century was a major watershed in the development of the pattern of landownership in Scotland.

In the 17th century, the increases in the numbers of landowners that had characterised the pattern during the preceding centuries ceased and the trend became reversed. A decline in the number of landowners was the conspicuous trend by the second half of the 17th century and this re-concentration of the ownership of land into fewer and fewer hands was to continue throughout the 18th and into the 19th century.

The beginning of this decline in the number of landowners reflected a shift during the 17th century in the balance between the main factors determining the power behind landownership. The change can be characterised as a rise in the economic over the military significance of land. Traditionally, bonds of kinship and the authority of feudal lordship had been the dominant influences in the values of land. During the 17th century kinship was still strong between landowners, but it was declining in importance and, at the same time, the role of feudal superiorities was also decreasing. Instead, the economic potential of land through rents and teinds was assuming a new priority in landownership.

One consequence of this change was that during the 17th century landowners became a more unified social and economic class. The distinction was reduced between tenants-in-chief and other feudal superiors and landowners holding by feu charter from a superior. While the authority of one over the other declined, they also came to share more in common as the proprietors of land. One element of this was the new roles for landowners in public administration, not least as Heritors or the owners of heritable property. By contrast with the closing gaps between different types of landowners, a more marked gulf was developing between landowners and non-landowners or the tenant population.

The 17th century incorporated a new degree of stability and economic growth compared to the preceding centuries and promoted these changes in landownership. However, the military significance of landownership, although of declining importance, did not end. It survived into the 18th century with the risings of 1715 and 1745, until the abolition of wardholding in 1747 after the defeat of the Jacobites. The 17th century had a complex mixture of military and economic influences, but it emerges clearly as a century of transition in the development of the pattern of landownership.

The most prominent military ventures of the 17th century were associated with the Covenanters and the Civil War, together with the revolution of 1688. Most leading landowning families were caught up in these events, which had a marked effect on local patterns of landownership. The Earls of Huntly, chiefs of the main landowning family in Aberdeenshire, were one of the most important landowners in Scotland and illustrate how a noble's position could change. Their fortunes, as royalists and catholics, oscillated both with national issues and through more local events, like the burning of Frendraught House in 1630. The estates of the 6th Earl had been forfeited in 1594 with those of Errol and the other catholic earls. Then, in 1597, they were restored and in 1599 the 6th Earl was created the 1st Marquis of Huntly. He was subsequently outlawed and then imprisoned in connection with the burning of Frendraught and died in 1636. The 2nd Marquis was beheaded as a royalist in 1649 and the estates again lost. The 3rd Marquis never regained the estates, which had fallen to the Earls of Argyll, before he died in 1653. In 1661, the Marquis of Argyll was executed and the estates were restored by Charles II to the underage 4th Marquis. In 1684, the 4th Marquis was created the 1st Duke of Gordon with the new grant of regality over his lands and vassals. However, by the end of the century, he was in prison as a suspected supporter of the deposed James VII.

Violent conflict was still common in the 17th century, but the growth in stability and, in some measure, prosperity could be seen in the changing architecture of the landowners' homes. The distinctive phase of 16th century castle building in the North-east ended during the 17th century and the last fortified house in Scotland, Leslie Castle in Aberdeenshire, had been built by 1661. In the early 17th century, other Aberdeenshire castles like Huntly and Drum were having substantial and comfortable residential blocks added. New buildings like William Forbes' Craigievar only resembled a castle in form while, by the end of the century, the 1st Earl of Kintore was having landscaped gardens laid out around his recently completed country mansion, Keith Hall.

The changed times were indicated by many other developments, including the amount of legislation dealing with land. In the first half of the century, these laws dealt mainly with questions of property and were aimed at consolidating landowners' possession of their lands. This legislation included prescriptions of hereditary rights and clarifications of titles, mainly aimed at tidying up and rationalising the sometimes confused legacy of the many earlier feudal grants. These grants had often been loose and ill-defined and, in some cases, the Crown had mistakenly granted overlapping areas to different proprietors.

One important initiative amongst the changing arrangements governing landownership, was the establishment of the Register of Sasines in 1617. This provided a central register in Edinburgh and registers in each county, where transactions in land could be recorded. The addition of these registers to the ritualised exchanges traditionally associated with any land transfer, provided a permanent record that could be consulted subsequently to validate titles and resolve any confusions over ownership.

A famous example of the problems that could arise over ownership, was the long-running question of the Earldom of Mar and Lordship of Garioch. After nearly 200 years, the Erskines had successfully established their claim to these titles in 1565. With the titles, they had regained the lands still held by the Crown in Deeside and Donside. However many of the lands belonging to these titles had been alienated by the Crown and its grantees of the preceding centuries. The reinstated Earls, while they agreed not to pursue their claims to some of these, notably Cluny and the Cabrach, started in 1587 to try and regain the rest. Eventually, in 1626, after a four year law case, the Earl of Mar successfully regained Kildrummy Castle and estate from Lord Elphinstone, whose family had been in possession there for over 110 years. In 1628, the Earl then proceeded with a legal action over the remaining lands held by over 150 proprietors.

Great attention was paid to the Mar cases throughout Scotland because of their potential implications. Many of the families involved in the dispute had been in possession of their lands for generations and included such prominent landowners as the Earl Marischal, the Lords Forbes, Deskford and Wemyss, the Irvines of Drum, Burnetts of Leys and Leslies of Balquhain, as well as many branches of the Gordons, Forbes, Leslies and Leiths. The threat posed by the claims caused great consternation and deep rummaging in the family charter chests. At the end of the day, most of the contestants survived in their lands, with the superiorities being found to belong to the Earls of Mar. The case was, however, the major instance of the application of the laws of feudal tenure in its day. It was a good example of the incentive to landowners to ensure that their titles to their lands were secure and of the type of situations which led to much of the early 17th century legislation.

The interest in titles reflected the concern of smaller landowners to secure the possession of their lands against the power of larger landowners. Confidence in titles and the possession of lands was also a requirement of the active land market during the 17th century. A particular feature of the period was the role of debts and bankruptcies in increasing the number of land transfers. This was not simply because heavily indebted landowners might have to sell their lands, but because lands could be lost by apprisal. Under this system, the debts of a landowner could be bought up from the creditors by another individual who was then entitled to claim the property. This process of apprisal was favoured not only by those who managed to acquire land through it, but also by the creditors who received payment of the debts sooner than would otherwise have been the case. The importance of apprisals has been illustrated by a survey of 17th century land transactions, which found that a third of these involved apprisals. Many major families, including most nobles, were falling into financial difficulties and their concern led to Acts in 1621, 1658, 1661 and 1672. These laws were designed to limit the use of apprisal as a method by which landowners could lose their lands. These laws also led to the introduction of the laws of entail in 1685, which safeguarded 'entailed' lands from forced sales through debts. The practise of entailing estates became steadily more widespread because, by securing the line of succession to an estate, it prevented the lands being broken up, even if an individual owner suffered bankruptcy, madness, imprisonment or some other major misfortune.

Sales of lands because of debts and the loss of lands through apprisals were a particularly prominent feature of the landmarket during the period of the Commonwealth in the mid 17th century. The financial position of many landowners had been weakened by heavy taxation, the destruction of property and borrowing. Royalists who had borrowed money to support their cause, usually from wealthy burgesses, were particularly indebted. The 4th Earl of Mar's son was one example and he ended up selling off much of the land which had been so hard won through the courts. The fortunes of the Huntly lands at this time also involved the issue of debts. When the Marquis of Argyll received the forfeited Huntly lands from the Covenanters in the 1640s, he proceeded to buy up the right to the many debts owed by the Earl of Huntly. Argyll hoped that, even if his right to the Huntly lands through the gift of a revolutionary government was subsequently overturned, he would still have a good claim to the lands in payment of Huntly's debts now owed to him. Argyll planned to pay off the debts out of the revenue he would be able to extract from the Huntly lands under his possession. However, the plan backfired. At the Restoration in 1661, the Argyll lands were forfeited and the Earls of Huntly were reinstated in their lands. Further, even though the Argyll lands were restored in 1663, the family was still out of favour and deemed to be still liable for the Huntly debts they had acquired.

The Restoration was widely welcomed in Scotland and marked the beginning of greater stability and increased economic activity. Confidence returned to the land market and, from this period, the long term decline in the numbers of landowners becomes conspicuous. The lack of adequate historical records means that it is not possible to date the start of this trend. The trend is likely, in any event, to have emerged at different dates in different localities. It is also probable that the re-concentration of landownership started during the first half of the 17th century and was temporarily reversed during the unsettled period from 1638 to 1660, after which it was quickly re-established.

It is possible to follow the subsequent decline in the number of landowners in some detail because of the fuller records of landownership that start to become available for Scotland's counties from the mid 17th century. These records are provided by valuation or tax rolls. The valuation rolls were based on the system of 'valued rent', which was first introduced in 1643 and continued to be used into the 19th century. The valued rent became represented by the real value of each property as valued in 1656. This fixed value became increasingly divorced from real money values as time passed, but it continued to provide the basis of assessment and provides a consistent valuation for comparisons for a period of nearly two centuries.

The valuation rolls were compiled for each parish and the landowners in that parish (the parish heritors) were listed along with the valued

Fig 3.1   Number of Parish Heritors in Aberdeenshire 1667

Districts	Modern Acreage	No of parishes	Total no of parish heritors	Average no of parish heritors	Total valued rent (££s Scots)	Average per parish heritor (££s Scots)
1. Deeside & Alford	574,155	23	246	10.7	59,658	242.5
2. Huntly & Garioch	208,871	22	194	8.8	48,086	247.9
3. Turriff, Ellon & Deer	375,951	26	259	10.0	116,688	450.5
4. Aberdeen	95,161	11	100	9.1	26,632	266.3
Aberdeenshire	1,254,138	82	799	9.7	251,064	314.2

rent of the land they owned there. Aberdeenshire is one of the first counties for which these records survive. In 1667, the first year for which a comprehensive valuation roll is available, there were 799 parish heritors in Aberdeenshire, sharing a total valued rent of over a quarter of a million pounds (Scots). The pattern of parish heritors, an average of 9.7 per parish, was fairly consistent throughout the county (Fig 3.1). The higher valued rent for the districts of Buchan reflected the greater agricultural worth of land there.

The number of parish heritors recorded for Aberdeenshire in 1667 was greater than the actual number of landowners in the county. In all counties, the larger landowners tended to hold land in more than one parish and so appeared more than once amongst the list of parish heritors. Removing this duplication reveals that there were 621 landowners in Aberdeenshire in 1667. Fig 3.2 shows the distribution of the counties valued rent between these landowners.

The pattern was dominated by relatively few large landowners. For example, 8.1% of the landowners (the 51 largest) held 44% of the county's valued rent between them, while 81% (the smallest 503) held 35.3%. This distribution also disguises the fact that, because the valued rent tended to be disproportionately higher on smaller estates, the larger landowners would have held a greater proportion of the county's land area than is indicated by their share of the valued rent.

These landowners have been classified for convenience into three broad classes. The Great Landlords were mainly composed of nobles or the titled aristocracy. They usually held their lands directly from the Crown with no intermediary feudal superiors. They accounted for the majority of the parish heritors occurring in more than one parish and derived most of their wealth from their extensive estates. The lairds

Fig 3.2   The Structure of Landownership in Aberdeenshire 1667

Class of Landowner	Estate Valuation (££s Scots)	Number in Class	Percentage of total no of Landowners	Percentage of total County Valuation
Great Landlords {	over £4,000	4 } 21	0.6 } 3.3	9.6 } 27.5
	£2,000-4,000	17	2.7	17.9
Lairds {	£1,000-2,000	30 } 97	4.8 } 15.6	16.5 } 35.5
	£500-1,000	67	10.8	19.0
Small Landowners {	£100-500	314 } 503	50.7 } 81.1	30.6 } 35.3
	up to £100	189	30.4	4.7
Kirklands, Institutions & Corporations	—	—	—	1.8
Totals		621	100%	(100%)

were a more diverse group both in their backgrounds and their sources of income which could come from, for example, professional positions and government posts as well as rents. The small landowners were more equivalent to the modern owner-occupier and included the 'Bonnet Lairds', which has become a traditional label for Scotland's smaller landowners. Many owed their existence to the feuing of small parcels of land by the Crown and Church. However, some could claim an equal pedigree of title to their noble superiors. For example, the Malcolms of Kinminity in the Aberdeenshire parish of Birse, whose valued rent was only £33. They had received these lands in the 11th century as a direct grant from King Malcolm III, after one of their ancestors caught the King's horse when it bolted in battle.

Fig 3.2 shows that the increases in the numbers of landowners before the 17th century had had relatively little effect on the structure of landownership in Aberdeenshire. Fig 3.3 shows that by 1667 there had also been little change in the composition of the main landowning families from those that had dominated landowning in Aberdeenshire during the previous centuries. Ten of the 25 largest landowners in 1667 were either Gordons (4) or Forbes (6) and there were only 12 family names between the top 25. Twenty out of the 25 were members of the same families that had dominated landownership in Aberdeenshire since the 14th century. These families, the Gordons, Forbes, Frasers, Erskines, Keiths, Hays and Irvines also had over 100 other landowning

Landownership in Scotland

Fig 3.3 The 25 Largest Landowners in Aberdeenshire 1667

Valued Rent (££ Scots)

1.	Gilbert Hay, Earl of Erroll	£9,168
2.	William Keith, 7th Earl Marischal	£6,542
3.	George Gordon, 4th Marquis of Huntly	£4,380
4.	Alexander Fraser, of Philorth, later Lord Saltoun	£4,300
5.	George Maule, 2nd Earl of Panmure	£3,700
6.	Mary Erskine, widow of 6th Earl Marischal	£3,659
7.	Alexander Forbes, Lord Pitsligo	£3,600
8.	Sir Alexander Forbes of Tolquhoun	£3,104
9.	Robert Irvine of Fedderat	£2,779
10.	Alexander Udny of Udny	£2,743
11.	John Erskine, Earl of Mar	£2,659
12.	Alexander Irvine of Drum	£2,544
13.	Sir Alexander Keith of Ludquharn	£2,541
14.	Andrew Fraser, Lord Fraser	£2,486
15.	Sir John Forbes, Baronet of Monymusk	£2,436
16.	Sir George Gordon of Haddo, later Earl of Aberdeen	£2,433
17.	Sir John Forbes of Watertoun	£2,321
18.	William Forbes, Master of Forbes	£2,164
19.	William Moir of Hilton	£2,133
20.	Charles Seton, Lord Fyvie, Earl of Dunfermline	£2,100
21.	Thomas Fraser, Laird of Strichen	£2,038
22.	Sir John Forbes of Craigievar	£1,850
23.	Adam Urquhart of Meldrum	£1,842
24.	Charles Gordon, Earl of Aboyne	£1,839
25.	Sir Ludovick Gordon of Terpersie	£1,813

branches between them in Aberdeenshire in 1667. Amongst the other 5 of the 25 largest landowners, the Udnys and Urquharts were both traditional Aberdeenshire landowning families.

The only new elements in the 1667 list were the Earls of Dunfermline and Panmure, and William Moir. Both these earldoms had been new 17th century creations and their lands in Aberdeenshire represented the expansion of these families beyond the areas where they had previously been landowners. The nobility had been expanded rapidly in the 17th century by the establishment of new earldoms. The Earl of Panmure, who had been elevated in 1646 after a career in trade and court service, exemplified the new nobles. They owed their position to government service and new wealth, rather than the inherited status of the older nobility. The other exception in 1667, William Moir, also reflected the changing times. He was an Aberdeen advocate whose success had enabled him to buy lands from the Urquharts and the Forbes.

The main Aberdeenshire landowning families in this list were all inter-related through marriage and linked together by a web of kinship that had built up over many generations. These kinship ties also spread down into the other important Aberdeenshire families not in the list. These included the Burnetts, Farquharsons, Leslies, Leiths and Innes, who between them held extensive territories and had about fifty landowning branches. There was also a range of smaller families, like the Meldrums and Menzies. In total, something around 25 family groups directly embraced nearly a third of all Aberdeenshire's 621 landowners and controlled more than two thirds of the country's valuation. These groups, apart from their own kinship connections, were also inter-related with many of the county's other landowners. This kinship cohesion, involving such a majority of the county's landowners, tended to be tighter the further up the social scale a family's position. The Great Landlords themselves were particularly intimately inter-related. An example is Mary Erskine, the only woman in the list of Aberdeenshire's top 25 landowners. She was herself sixth in the rating, sister to the Earl of Mar (eleventh), mother of the 7th Earl Marischal (second) and also step-mother to the 2nd Earl of Panmure (fifth). This 2nd Earl had just inherited his title in 1661 when the 1st Earl died. The first Earl had been married to Mary Erskine for twenty five years, though she was his third wife and he was her second husband.

The conspicuous domination of the pattern of landownership in Aberdeenshire in 1667 by the Great Landlords and their kinship groups increased further with the decline in the number of landowners during the following decades.

The average number of parish heritors in Aberdeenshire dropped from 9.7 in 1667 to 8.9 in 1674 and was down to 7.0 by 1696. This represented a reduction in the total number of parish heritors in the county by a quarter in 30 years. This decline occurred in every district of the county, though it was greatest in the more arable areas and in the areas that had had the most heritors in 1667. A quarter of the parishes showed no change during this period, but these were parishes that already had an average of less than four heritors each, well under the county average. Two thirds of Aberdeenshire's parishes did show a reduction and only half a dozen out of 82 showed an increase. Even amongst these, the increase was invariably only by one heritor.

While the number of heritors declined by over 25% between 1667 and 1696, there was an even greater reduction in the actual number of landowners. The re-concentration of landownership meant that a larger proportion of the remaining landowners held land in several parishes. Most of the 100 largest landowners expanded their estates during this period and families like the Forbes, who started to decline from their zenith, were the exceptions. The share of the county's valued rent held by these 100 landowners increased to well over 50%, with the greatest gains made by some of the previously middle ranking families, like the Farquharsons and Leiths.

This expansion by the larger landowners was at the expense of smaller landowners, whose numbers showed a steep decline. Most often these small landowners were the families who had joined the ranks of the landowners during the previous increases in the number of landowners in the county. The re-concentration also reflected a decline in the practise of landowners making over separate property to various sons and the growing tendency for all of a family's lands to be concentrated under one main line.

The re-concentration of landownership was only a net trend. The advantages of landownership meant that there was a growing number of outsiders in the land market, particularly for smaller estates, and this tended in part to counter the re-concentration of landownership amongst the existing landowners. This demand was most significant in the parishes closest to Aberdeen. The newcomers, who might themselves be the younger sons of landowners, came from several up and coming income groups that reflected the increased economic activity in Scottish society in the late 17th century. The majority of these new landowners came from mercantile backgrounds, while the next largest group was from the legal profession. The backgrounds of the remainder were mainly military, church, public service or, in a county like Aberdeenshire, the universities.

The larger landowners were, however, still the main source of capital in the country and dominated the land market. These land-owners' direct purchases were often through the agency of debts, particularly in the lean years of the 1690s. Many small landowners fell into difficulties at that time, with some forced to exchange their feu for a tenancy in return for the next year's seed corn during the famine. The resumption of feus was also another important means by which landowners increased or consolidated their estates. Feudal superiors were able to re-acquire lands when their vassals came to obtain a new title, a power still reflected in modern superiors' rights of pre-emption. In the 17th century, when feu holders had considerably less rights than a modern feudal vassal, the resumption of these previously granted lands enabled the larger landowners to reassemble territories that had become fragmented. This practise was widely resented in the 17th century and has many parallels in the recent trend of landowners to take tenanted farmland 'in-hand'. In the 17th century, the value of fixed rent feus had been eroded by inflation and land could be more profitably managed directly through tenancies with rents that could be increased to maintain their maximum value.

The consolidation and expansion of their estates by the larger landowners during the second half of the 17th century, reflected the new profits that could be derived from land. The legislation of the Scots Parliament relating to land also reflected this new interest. Acts during the first half of the 17th century had mainly been concerned with strengthening the institution of private property. During the second half of the century, an increasing number of Acts were concerned with changes on the land itself. For example, the Acts dealing with winter herding, estate marches, commonties and runrig lands.

The change towards the direct economic management of estate lands was also illustrated by the re-organisations taking place on the estates themselves. These changes involved building up estate admini-stration and restructuring the tenant population. Prominent amongst this restructuring was the conversion of multiple tenancies into single tenant holdings, with each tenant having their own lease for a separate unit. On all holdings, written leases on set terms were increasingly used to replace verbal agreements.

By the end of the 17th century these changes had made varying progress in different districts and some changes, like converting rents to cash from kind, could be locally and temporarily reversed by adverse circumstances such as those in the 1690s. In Aberdeenshire, the extent of the changes is illustrated by the pattern of single and multiple tenancies in 1696. The progress to single tenancies was greatest on the richer lands of the Garioch, the Deveron and Ythan valleys and in the hinterlands of Aberdeen. This meant that in the east of the county 50-70% of the farms were single tenancies. In the parishes along the Highland:Lowland divide across the county this figure was 30-50%, while in the upland districts of western Aberdeen-shire less than 30% of the farms had been converted to single tenancies.

These organisational changes by landowners on their estates had been preceded by the earlier concerns of landowners with their land as property. Similarly, these changes in estate administration occurred in advance of the technical innovations, such as liming and crop rotations, that were to have a major impact on agricultural development during the 18th century. The 17th century changes increased the landowners' incomes from the existing resources, compared with the subsequent strategy of improving the resource as a method of increasing incomes. In Highland districts, this was reflected by the sharp rise in the commercial exploitation of the existing native woodlands in the 17th century, with estate forestry not emerging until the 18th century.

The externally based exploitation of the Caledonian forests started in the west, central and eastern Highlands at the beginning of the 17th century and resulted from timber and fuelwood shortages in England and Lowland Scotland. This penetration of the Highlands by commercial interests was also accompanied by the rise of the drove trade to export cattle to southern markets.

These developments were part of the transition in the 17th century. Landuse, rather than simply land, had become more clearly established as the basis of profitable estate management. The 17th century was also a land hungry century, with cultivation and settlement spreading on to new sites or, at least in some instances, sites which had not been used for centuries, sometimes not since the Bronze Age. Scotland's population had risen to around one million by the late 17th century with over half the population north of the Tay and over 80% of the people living on the land.

The population was severely affected by the ill years of the 1690s, when a run of freak seasons and a succession of crop failures reduced the population in many areas by up to 25% or more. At the same time, the depressed Scottish economy was hard hit by the collapse by 1700 of the Darien Scheme, which had hoped to set up a Scots Colony in Panama. These were the prevailing conditions as Scotland moved towards a Union of Parliaments with England.

At this time, there were around 9,500 landowners in Scotland, only about half of whom had the right to inherit or sell the land they held. Amongst these landowners, the Great Landowners with their kinship groups were dominant. The importance of these powerful landowners in the affairs of Scotland during the 17th century is hard to over-estimate.

Chapter 4

The 18th Century

The close relationship that had always existed in Scotland between power and landownership continued throughout the 18th century. There were many important changes in Scotland during the century, but the major landowners still dominated the country's economic, social and political life.

The pattern of landownership during the 18th century followed the same trend as had emerged in the 17th century. Fewer and fewer people owned Scotland's land as the estates of the larger landowners continued to grow and the number of smaller landowners declined further. Many factors influenced the overall rates at which these changes occurred, but there were only very local exceptions to this national trend and these were principally in the parishes around Scotland's major towns.

The fortunes of agriculture, by far Scotland's major industry throughout the century, were a central influence on the re-concentration of landownership. However, as reflected in the beginnings of this re-concentration during the 17th century, the rate of re-concentration in the 18th century was greatest in the decades before Improvement became widespread. In Aberdeenshire and most counties, the techniques of Improvement, such as drainage, liming, crop rotations, enclosure, improved implements and stock breeding, only became fully established after 1770. Yet, by that time, the number of landowners in Aberdeenshire was already down to one third of the number 100 years before.

The reduction in the number of landowners during the 18th century did not follow a regular progression. In the opening decades, the agricultural depression of the 1690s and the surpluses that followed, together with the political uncertainties surrounding the Union of 1707 and the Jacobite Rising of 1715, were dominant factors. In these circumstances, the average number of parish heritors in Aberdeenshire stayed fairly constant. In some areas of the county, the decline in the number of parish heritors was reversed slightly and the overall county average of 7.0 in 1696 was 7.3 by 1715.

The decline in the number of Aberdeenshire's landowners resumed during the 1720s and 1730s and the average number of parish heritors was down to 6.5 by 1741. The first conspicuous examples of innovative developments in landuse practises and rural development strategies occurred during these decades. The most prominent of the early improvers in Aberdeenshire was Sir Archibald Grant of Monymusk. His operations began in the early 1730s and, like many of the other pioneers in that period, he had spent time in England and employed Englishmen to help run his estate. Another Aberdeenshire improver was Joseph Cumine, who established the county's first planned village at Cuminestown in 1739.

The Jacobite Rebellion of 1745 was a dramatic indication of the uncertain times that still prevailed in the 1740s. As earlier in the century, the average number of parish heritors in Aberdeenshire oscillated slightly and was 6.7 by 1754. Many of Aberdeenshire's landowning families were once again involved in this third Jacobite rebellion. The defeat of the rebellion was followed in 1747 by several important changes in Scotland's feudal land tenure. These reforms, instigated by the government in London, included the abolition of wardholding and buying out some of the heritable jurisdictions still possessed by feudal landlords for £152,000. The possessors of feu charters were also given the right to sell their land to the person of their choice, without having to obtain their superior's permission.

These feudal reforms did not alter the pattern of landownership in Scotland, but they were a further step in unifying landowners into a single class of property owners. Feudal superiors could still reserve rights and impose burdens, but the wider influence of superiorities had become limited to parliamentary representation. At the same time, landowners below the ranks of the Great Landlords were increasingly influential through their roles in county and local administrations.

The '45 was the last of the military episodes of factions and forfeitures that had characterised the previous centuries of feudal landownership in Scotland. Following the defeat of the rebellion and the restoration of confidence, the number of parish heritors fell sharply and the average for Aberdeenshire was 5.5 in 1771. The decrease in this average from 9.7 in 1667, represented an overall reduction in the

Fig 4.1   The Number of Parish Heritors in Aberdeenshire
1667 and 1771

District	Number of Parishes	Total Number of Parish Heritors		Average per Parish	
		1667	1771	1667	1771
1. Deeside & Alford	23	246	128	10.7	5.6
2. Huntly & Garioch	22	194	98	8.8	4.5
3. Turriff, Ellon & Deer	26	259	146	10.0	5.6
4. Aberdeen	11	100	76	8.8	6.9
Aberdeenshire	82	799	448	9.7	5.5

total number of parish heritors in the county from 799 to 448 between 1667 and 1771.

Fig 4.1 shows the distribution of this decline between the districts of Aberdeenshire. The smallest reduction was in the Aberdeen district where, unlike the other areas, the number of heritors had increased since the 1690s due to the proximity of Aberdeen.

The actual number of landowners in Aberdeenshire decreased from 621 to 250 between 1667 and 1771. This was a much greater reduction than in the total number of parish heritors because, as the pattern of landownership became more concentrated, an increasing percentage of landowners had lands in more than one parish. By 1771, nearly a third (74) of Aberdeenshire's landowners held land in more than one of the county's parishes. The greatest of these was the Earl of Aberdeen, whose estates encompassed lands in 18 parishes, and he also owned land in East Lothian. Thirteen of Aberdeenshire's other landowners in 1771 also owned important estates outside the county. These landowners were almost exclusively from the ranks of the Great Landlords and their other estates were scattered throughout the nearby counties of Angus, Kincardine, Banff, Moray and Inverness.

Fig 4.2 shows how the structure of landownership had changed during this decline in the number of landowners. The share of the Great Landlords had steadily increased and by 1771, 27 of them owned half the county. Despite this increase, the extent held by lairds with lands worth £1,000-2,000 (Scots) had stayed quite constant: 35.5% in 1667 and 32.8% in 1771. Similarly, the overall number of landowners amongst these lairds and the Great Landlords had hardly changed: 119 in 1667 and 114 in 1771. The changes that had occurred in the numbers of landowners and the growth of the Great Landlords' estates had

Fig 4.2   The Structure of Landownership in Aberdeenshire 1771

Class of Landowner	Estate Valuation (££s Scots)	Number in Class	Percentage of total no of Landowners	Percentage of total County Valuation
Great Landlords {	over £4,000	9	3.6	28.4
	£2,000-4,000	18 } 27	7.2 } 10.8	21.2 } 49.6
Lairds {	£1,000-2,000	30	12.0	17.1
	£500-1,000	53 } 83	21.2 } 33.2	15.8 } 32.9
Small Landowners {	£100-500	89	35.6	11.0
	up to £100	51 } 140	20.4 } 56.0	1.3 } 12.3
Kirklands, Institutions & Corporations	—	—	—	5.2
Totals		250	100%	(100%)

been almost entirely at the expense of the small landowners. Their number fell by 363 to just 140 between 1667-1771 and their percentage of the county dropped by 23% to 12.3%.

The structure of Aberdeenshire's landownership is also shown in Fig 4.3, where the contraction at the base of the pattern by 1771 compared to 1667 is clearly illustrated. In Fig 4.4, the straightforward progression of a few individuals owning a large percentage of the county is shown with, for example, 90% held by just 133 of the 250 landowners and 50% held by only 27 individuals.

This concentrated pattern of landownership in Aberdeenshire was not unusual in Scotland. Fig 4.5 lists the percentage of each county held by the Great Landlords, Lairds and smallest landowners or Bonnet Lairds. This shows how Aberdeenshire fitted into the wider pattern of landownership in Scotland as a whole. The overall control of Scotland's land by the Great Landlords was most complete in the Borders, at around 65%, and up the east coast, 40-50%. The Great Landlords also dominated the Highlands, although the figures for each county were influenced by the extent of forfeited estates held by the government. In all these three broad geographic areas, the Bonnet Lairds never held so much as 10%. The exception in this overall pattern was the west and central region, where the Great Landlords never owned more than 35%. In these counties, the Bonnet Lairds were most numerous

*Fig 4.3   Changes in the Structure of Landownership in Aberdeenshire
1667 to 1771*

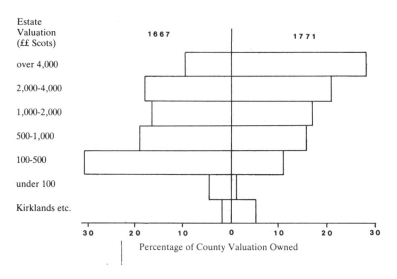

Estate
Valuation
(££ Scots)

over 4,000

2,000-4,000

1,000-2,000

500-1,000

100-500

under 100

Kirklands etc.

1667   1771

30   20   10   0   10   20   30

Percentage of County Valuation Owned

*Fig 4.4   Percentages of Aberdeenshire Owned by the
Largest Landowners in 1771*

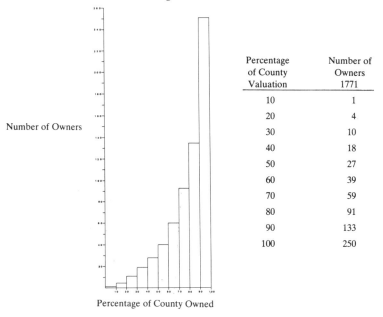

Number of Owners

Percentage of County Owned

Percentage of County Valuation	Number of Owners 1771
10	1
20	4
30	10
40	18
50	27
60	39
70	59
80	91
90	133
100	250

49

Landownership in Scotland

Fig 4.5   Landownership in Scotland, 1771
The percentage of the valued rent of each county controlled by landowners with estates in that county valued at:

County	Over £2000 (Scots) (Great Landlords)	£100-£2000 (Scots) (Lairds)	Under £100 (Scots) (Bonnet Lairds)
Aberdeen	50.0	44.2	1.3
Angus	49.7	46.2	3.0
Argyll	46.0	51.2	1.9
Ayr	34.1	54.9	10.2
Banff	26.2	64.8	6.0
Berwick	50.5	48.5	3.5
Bute	52.8	38.1	9.1
Caithness	44.4	47.3	1.6
Clackmannan	22.1	64.6	13.3
Dumfries	65.7	27.6	6.7
Dumbarton	19.5	60.5	15.7
East Lothian	69.7	26.7	1.4
Fife	44.4	48.7	3.7
Inverness	40.8	39.9	3.8
Kincardine	39.7	50.0	0.5
Kinross	0	77.5	20.3
Kirkcudbright	39.1	54.9	3.6
Lanark	27.8	54.0	13.5
Midlothian	40.8	53.9	3.7
Moray	57.6	39.0	1.2
Nairn	55.8	42.3	1.2
Orkney	54.1	38.7	7.1
Peebles	41.0	50.7	2.8
Perth	41.4	47.7	5.1
Renfrew	26.8	62.7	8.2
Ross & Cromarty	40.0	50.1	0.9
Roxburgh	73.6	22.0	5.4
Selkirk	65.1	33.6	0
Stirling	9.4	68.4	13.7
Sutherland	67.7	31.6	0.7
West Lothian	53.2	42.4	4.4
Wigtown	49.4	45.3	3.8
Average for counties	43.7	47.7	5.5%
Range between counties	0-73.6%	22.0-77.5%	0-20.3%

(After Timperley 1977)

Fig 4.6   Titles amongst the Great Landlords 1771

	Estates valued at more than £4000 (Scots)		Estates valued at £2000-£4000 (Scots)	
	Scotland	Aberdeen	Scotland	Aberdeen
Duke	9	1	—	—
Earl	33	4	7	1
Countess	1	—	1	1
Marquis	3	—	—	—
Viscount	3	—	—	—
Lord	12	—	10	—
Lady	2	—	—	—
Baronet	18	1	42	1
Total with Titles	81	6	60	3
No Title	42	3	126	15
Total	123	9	186	18

(After Timperley 1977)

and this was a direct consequence of the 16th and 17th century feuing of Church and Crown lands in small parcels. The Crown was still an important Scottish landowner in 1771, even if not conspicuous in Aberdeenshire. The Crown had lands in twelve counties and was the 19th largest landowner in Scotland, with a valued rent of over £20,000 (Scots). Most of these lands appear to have been lost by the Crown under George III (1760-1820) in exchange for the Civil List.

The Great Landlords, who dominated this overall pattern of landownership, still included most of Scotland's noble or aristocratic families, as illustrated in Fig 4.6. Two thirds of the Great Landlords with lands over £4,000 (Scots) were titled, both in Scotland and within Aberdeenshire. The Great Landlords with estates valued between £2,000-£4,000 (Scots) were however, less titled in Aberdeenshire than Scotland as a whole. The proportions of titles amongst all the Great Landlords of Aberdeenshire had declined from two thirds in 1667 to one third in 1771. This reflected that, although the Great Landlords had nearly doubled their share of the county during that century, there had been some notable changes in their ranks. Over 17 of the top 25 owners in 1667 had suffered the complete loss or substantial reduction of their estates by 1771 due to either military or financial failure.

Fig 4.7   The 25 Largest Landowners in Aberdeenshire 1771

	Valued Rent (££ Scots)
1. William Gordon, Earl of Aberdeen	£21,605
2. Alexander Gordon, Duke of Gordon	£10,396
3. James Hay, Earl of Erroll	£ 7,584
4. George Keith, 10th Earl Marischal	£ 5,684
5. James Ferguson of Pitfour	£ 4,524
6. Sir William Forbes of Craigievar	£ 4,436
7. General Horn of Logie	£ 4,400
8. James Duff, 2nd Earl Fife	£ 4,345
9. Alexander Garden of Troup	£ 4,125
10. Charles Gordon, Earl of Aboyne	£ 3,719
11. James Farquharson of Invercauld	£ 3,535
12. Alexander Udny of Udny	£ 3,158
13. George Fraser, Lord Saltoun	£ 3,093
14. Alexander Fraser of Strichen	£ 3,072
15. Alexander Leith of Leithhall	£ 3,071
16. John Duff of Hatton	£ 2,996
17. Sir Archibald Grant of Monymusk	£ 2,909
18. Robert Gordon of Esslemont and Hallhead	£ 2,887
19. Alexander Leith of Freefield	£ 2,839
20. Andrew Skene of Dyce	£ 2,724
21. Francis Farquharson of Finzean	£ 2,497
22. Heirs of Patrick Duff of Premnay	£ 2,460
23. Colonel William Gordon of Fyvie	£ 2,338
24. John Grant of Rothmaise	£ 2,327
25. John Leslie of Balquhain	£ 2,217

Each of the three Jacobite risings had had a direct influence on the composition of Aberdeenshire's top landowners in 1771 (Fig 4.7). In 1690, the Earl of Dunfermline's lands were forfeited and in 1715 the same happened to the estates of the Earls of Mar, Marischal and Panmure. These estates were subsequently sold at bargain prices with, for example, James Ferguson of Pitfour acquiring the Marischal estates and Lord Braco (Earls of Fife) the Mar estates. The 10th Earl Marischal, who had his estates forfeited, appears in the 1771 list because he later fell heir to the Earl of Kintore's estates, but the Earl Marischal never settled in Scotland again after 1715.

As a result of the 1745 Rising, around 50 estates were forfeited in Scotland. Many of these soon came back to their owners or the owners' families, but in 1752 thirteen of them were annexed by the government and their management handed over to the Forfeited

Estates Commissioners. The holding of these estates, worth £35,595 valued rent in 1771, meant that the Government was the fourteenth largest landowner in Scotland. This government holding significantly reduced the extent of some counties held by the Great Landlords, as with Inverness-shire where the Commissioners had six estates valued at £11,334.

The forfeited estates in Aberdeenshire included those of Lord Forbes of Pitsligo, Gordon of Glenbuchat, Gordon of Terpersie, Hay of Asleed, Farquharson of Monaltrie and Duguid of Auchinhove. The only one of these which was annexed was Monaltrie. Like all the other annexed estates, it was a Gaelic speaking community and may also have been chosen for its strategic river crossing. The Forfeited Estate Commissioners were pioneering improvers on the estates under their management, investing in roads and bridges, local industries, afforestation, farm re-organisation and other initiatives. Monaltrie was, however, the smallest of all the forfeited estates and was very little changed by annexation. The small-scale, poor tenants of Monaltrie even decided against the removal of the ancient bond of thirlage, as they feared this would lead to an increase in their rents. After thirteen years of formal annexation, Monaltrie was leased back to the Farquharsons and then in 1784, was returned to them as owners, as were all the other annexed estates.

The other main factor affecting the composition of Aberdeenshire's top landowners was the changing financial fortunes of the different families. Three top Forbes landowners all fell into money difficulties within a few years of each other. Forbes of Tolquhoun was bankrupted by the collapse of the Darien Scheme, while Forbes of Monymusk was bankrupt by 1713. Shortly afterwards, Lord Forbes lost his marriage dowry in the South Sea Scheme. For some of the other landowners, the financial problems were less sudden. The Earl of Errol was still in the top 25 in 1771, but his family's wealth was already steadily declining. They had complained bitterly when the Treaty of Union abolished most of the privileges and monetary dues associated with the Errols' hereditary position as Lord High Constable of Scotland. This and other factors, including their own unsettled descent or succession in the 18th century, were gradually eroding their estates. The same happened to the lands of the Irvines of Drum, but that was due to the pursuit of too many legal disputes, which included some of the most complex and expensive legal cases in Scotland during the 18th century.

The financial difficulties of some leading families resulted from a failure to adapt to the changing times, while others suffered from an over-extravagant involvement with them. In other cases, it was simply a product of the timing of generations, an old generation dying hard when a younger one might have taken the initiative with the new opportunities available. Whatever the cause, the financial pressures were always felt on the landowners' estates before they were allowed to affect the landowners' personal situation. The financial difficulties of major landowners could have a wide and long term impact, with a retarding effect on development throughout a locality covering several parishes. The laws of entail tended to promote this by preventing the sale of land even when the landowner was bankrupt.

There were however, other families whose fortunes were rising and who were always ready to absorb the lands of another, if they were not adequately protected by entail. The Gordons, for example, were expanding rapidly during the 18th century and it was the Earl of Aberdeen who acquired most of the Irvines of Drum lands. Such expansions could spread over several counties. The Duke of Gordon, although Aberdeenshire's second largest landowner, held a greater valuation of lands in the counties of Inverness, Banff and Moray. Similarly, the Grants, who acquired Monymusk from the Forbes, held extensive lands in those other counties. Another spectacular rise was by Garden of Troup, who expanded through a very profitable lease from the York Building Company between 1728-64. This particular Company occupies a distinctive niche in the history of Scottish landownership, although it had no influence on the pattern or trends. It was a London company with a commission to provide that city's water supply. It saw the sale of Jacobite estates as a potentially profitable investment opportunity and initiated major programmes of economic exploitation on the estates it acquired, including those in the Peterhead area. Before the end of the century, the Company's own financial difficulties had forced it to withdraw from landowning in Scotland.

The York Building Company was an exception. The lands lost by leading families were invariably acquired by old families moving up the ranks of the county's landowners. The changes that occurred were an interchange between the top and middling landowners. Families like the Forbes and Irvines might have dropped out of the top 25 through folly or misfortune, but they still remained important landowners. Similarly, it was not new families that appeared in their stead, but just other old families which were expanding. The Gordons obtained a clear dominance of the county, owning around 30% of its value between them. The next 40% below them was owned exclusively by Aberdeenshire's traditional landowning families. These were, in order of holding, the Forbes, Grants, Irvines, Burnetts and Leslies. Even General Horn who appears in the top 25, was of an old family, the Horns of Westhall and Pitmedden, and he had married into the Elphinstones of Logie.

The expansion of large estates and the domination by long established families in the 18th century were counteracted by an active land market. This demand operated mainly at the lower end of the estate structure and helped maintain a nucleus of small estates against the overall trend towards a more concentrated pattern of landownership. The people buying into land in the first half of the 18th century included several new groups compared with the late 17th century. Prominent amongst these were returned Scots who had made money in Europe and in more exotic new spheres like the East Indies, typically as soldiers or as merchants. These groups included many newcomers to Scotland's landed class but, as with the more traditional purchasers from the commercial sector and legal profession, they also included many younger sons of existing landed families.

The acquisition of land in the first half of the 18th century still involved speculation in bankruptcy by buying out 'wadsetters' (the holders of debt pledges), but the growth of the land market reflected an overall opening out of the Scottish money market. Both these markets grew strongly during the second half of the century as more financial factors came into play. The situation was reflected by land rents which had been stable for the first half of the century. Rents started to rise and climbed steeply after 1768, as the Scots pound disappeared through depreciation, so that they doubled between 1783-1793. The value of this increase was accentuated as interest rates were in general falling and estate rent rolls were expanding as new holdings were developed through Improvement. Rent rolls themselves, not just estates, were acceptable as real security on loans and the growth of the Scottish banking community made money both available and easy to borrow.

Major landowners were the traditional source of capital and they continued as a source of funds, not least for public enterprises like roads, bridges and harbours. Previously, failed investments had taken their toll amongst the larger landowners but, by the second half of the 18th century, many landowners were starting to derive important extra income from well-placed capital. Money was thus being lent to and by landowners so that it was not a question of whether money was being lent to or away from the land. The other groups who provided capital, merchants and bankers and the lawyers, who both lent money and played such an important role in organising financial arrangements, all tended to be acquiring property as part of their wealth. As prices rose with the passing of each decade, they were a steadily more conspicuous element in the landmarket. These incomers, in comparison with earlier in the century, had obtained their wealth within Scotland's increasingly active and diverse economy, rather than just being people who had earned their money abroad.

The growth of landowners' incomes from the new financial markets was important in the funding of agricultural changes. Improvement became widespread from the 1760s and, for example, had made some progress in virtually every Aberdeenshire parish by the end of the 18th century. Initially, improvements had tended to be just on landowners' home farms and policies. However, during the last quarter of the 18th century, the changes were spreading across the tenanted holdings and already the tenants were assuming the dominant position they were to have in the transformation of the landscape in Aberdeenshire and Scotland as a whole.

The improving landowners in the first half of the 18th century had been motivated by a mixture of patriotism, fashion and admiration of the English situation. However, during the second half of the century, this gave way to commercialism. Rents, land-uses and investments all offered strong returns to the landowners on their expenditures on estate improvements and public enterprises. The quest for profit motivated the spread of improvements. One consequence of this was the erosion of any sense of 'moral obligation' between landowner and tenant that might have survived from more clanish times. The new farm lay-outs, which accompanied enclosure, liming and rotations, were already displacing families from the land and, in upland Aberdeenshire, wholesale clearances for sheep farming had been occurring since the 1760s. The political gulf between the landowners and the local populace that was to surface in the 19th century was already conspicuous. Rural unrest against unjust power and authority was also encouraged by the examples of the French and American Revolutions. An eloquent statement of this discontent from Aberdeenshire, was Alexander Campbell's 'The Grampian's Desolate', written in the last years of the 18th century. It was a 300 page criticism of the fate of the rural North-east and advocated that landowners profits should be used for the benefit of displaced families. It also called for a comprehensive survey of landownership and landuses.

The strong economic and political position of landowners also incorporated rising expenses and commitments. The management of their households, as well as making provisions for their dependents, could all prove a serious drain on resources. The landowners, as heritors, also had parochial commitments to the buildings and staff of church and schools, and to poor relief. Some landowners also had expenditure on political lobbying and electioneering, and legal disputes were prevalent, particularly for dividing commonties and defining boundaries. On top of these, there was a growing tax burden from the government in London, not least to support its war efforts. Many landowners did successfully evade the Assessed Taxes of the late 18th century that levied rates on a diverse range of items from windows to watches. However, in 1799 William Pitt consolidated and enforced these into a single income tax that resulted in a sharp increase in the payments by landowners.

There was an inevitable variation in how the different landowning families fared in the economy of the last quarter of the 18th century. However, in Aberdeenshire, the sharp decline in the fortunes of Garden of Troup was an exception. Otherwise, there were only minor adjustments of ranking amongst Aberdeenshire's 50 or so main landowners and the average number of parish heritors in the county stayed constant at 5.5 in 1771 and 1791. However, there were important variations within the county.

Around Aberdeen, the number of parish heritors continued to increase as it had done for a century by then. In East Aberdeenshire, the pattern was more variable, but showed a significant change to an overall increase in parish heritors. In part, this resulted from particular increases in some areas, for example at Peterhead, where the lands of the York Building Company were sold when it collapsed. The main purchaser of these was the Merchant Company of Edinburgh, although it was still exceptional for businesses to own significant amounts of land in Aberdeenshire. A more important aspect of the change in East Aberdeenshire was an increase of heritors in some of the most agriculturally developed parishes. This was a trend that would emerge over the whole county during the next century.

The increases in the east of the county were, however, still exceeded by the continuing decline in parish heritors in the west of the county. These were the upland districts like Deeside and Garioch, which included the parishes where Improvement had made least progress. The net result was that the actual number of landowners in Aberdeenshire fell between 1771 and 1800 from 250 to 236. This was accompanied by a further small increase in estates of the larger landowners, so that by the end of the 18th century 63 individuals shared 70% of the county's total valuation.

The last quarter of the 18th century was a favourable period for

Fig 4.8   The 25 Largest Landowners in Aberdeenshire, 1802

Valued Rent (££ Scots)

1. George Gordon, 4th Earl of Aberdeen   £17,403
2. Alexander Gordon, 4th Duke of Gordon   £10,693
3. James Duff, 2nd Earl Fife   £ 9,221
4. Hon William Gordon of Ellon   £ 5,499
5. James Ferguson of Pitfour   £ 5,254
6. Sir William Forbes of Craigievar   £ 4,577
7. Robert Dalrymple Horn Elphinstone of Logie   £ 4,399
8. Charles Gordon, Earl of Aboyne   £ 4,042
9. John Robert Udny of Udny and Dudwick   £ 3,958
10. Anthony Keith-Falconer, Earl of Kintore   £ 3,725
11. Charles Gordon of Cluny   £ 3,657
12. Archibald Farquharson of Finzean   £ 3,603
13. James Farquharson of Invercauld   £ 3,588
14. Major-General Alexander Hay of Rannas   £ 3,194
15. William Hay, Earl of Erroll   £ 2,970
16. Sir Archibald Grant of Monymusk   £ 2,872
17. Robert William Duff of Fetteresso   £ 2,826
18. Andrew Skene of Dyce   £ 2,787
19. General Hon William Gordon of Fyvie   £ 2,618
20. Alexander Fraser, 16th Lord Saltoun   £ 2,454
21. Francis Farquharson of Haughton   £ 2,406
22. Harry Niven Lumsden of Auchindoir   £ 2,236
23. John Leslie of Balquhain   £ 2,217
24. Thomas Gordon of Buthlaw   £ 2,161
25. Theodore Morison of Bogney   £ 2,156

landowners and this was reflected in the limited changes in the composition of Aberdeenshire's top landowners by the beginning of the 19th century (Fig 4.8). Most of the new entries in the list (Nos 21, 22, 24 and 25) were only minor adjustments in ranking since 1771. For example, the Morisons of Bogney still held the same valuation as in 1771, while the Gordons of Buthlaw had increased their valuation through their money from Jamaica. The Hon William Gordon at No 4 in the list was a son of the 3rd Earl of Aberdeen, to whom the Earl's Ellon estate had been bequeathed. Two other changes in the top 25 also resulted from inheritance, Leith of Leith-Hall to Hay of Rannas and Duff of Premnay to Duff of Fetteresso. The other change was the entry of the longstanding landowners, Gordons of Cluny, at No 11 and this was the only example of a sharp rise in fortunes.

The trend towards fewer landowners and larger estates had occurred for around a century and a half by 1800 and was to continue into the

19th century. It was the trend for Scotland as a whole. Scotland had had around 9,500 landowners at the beginning of the 18th century, around 8,500 mid-century and about 8,000 at the start of the 19th century. During that period, Scotland's population had increased from around 1 million to 1½ million, so that the percentage of Scotland's population owning Scotland's lands had fallen from 1% to ½% of the total population.

The 18th century did see many changes in the circumstances of Scotland's major landowners. However, by the late 18th century, landownership had entered a highly profitable era. The powers that these major landowners had lost, for example through the Union of 1707 and the subsequent authority of a London based government, were countered by the extent of Scotland's land they had secured. The control of this land with all the political, social and economic values it still represented, allowed these landowners to retain their all-pervasive dominance of society in Scotland through into the 19th century.

Chapter 5

The 19th Century

The patterns of landownership in Aberdeenshire and Scotland as a whole remained more constant during the 19th century than during the 17th and 18th centuries. Throughout the 19th century, 90% of Aberdeenshire's area was owned by less than 15 landowners and 90% of Scotland by less than 1500 landowners.

Within this fairly constant 19th century pattern, the most significant change was an increase in the total number of landowners. Before the end of the century, this new trend had emerged throughout Scotland and was reversing the decline in landowners that had occurred since the 17th century. However, these new landowners tended to be small landowners and they had little overall effect on the pattern of large estates.

The decline in the number of landowners in Scotland had continued during the opening decades of the 19th century. The number fell from 8000 in 1800 to 7637 in 1814. This was a net decrease, with the number of small estates increasing near the burghs and cities, while the re-concentration of landownership continued in remoter districts and Highland counties.

The pattern of landownership in Aberdeenshire followed these trends. The number of landowners in the county was down to 230 by 1814, with a further small increase in the estates of the larger landowners (Fig 5.1). The most conspicuous concentration of ownership into fewer hands was in the uplands of West Aberdeenshire. In the east of the county, the trend varied with local circumstances and there were small net increases in owners around the burghs and in some areas of richer ground. In Aberdeen district the number of landowners continued to increase as much of the barren ground around the city was

Fig 5.1   The Number of Landowners by Valuation in
Aberdeenshire 1771, 1802, 1814

Valuation	Number of Landowners		
(££s Scots)	1771	1802	1814
over £2,000	27	27	28
£500-2,000	83	89	88
up to £500	140	120	114
Total	250	236	230

brought into production to supply the expanding urban population with milk and vegetables.

By the 1840s the county as a whole was showing a net increase in the total number of parish heritors (Fig 5.2). Deeside and Alford were the last districts to show this increase and this did not emerge until the mid 19th century. Similarly, these remoter upland areas were the last places where Improvement became widely adopted and both these trends spread across the county in a pattern that resembled the progress of single tenancies during the 17th century. By the mid 19th century, although some pockets remained relatively unaffected, Improvement was occurring throughout Aberdeenshire. The new horizons that had opened up for the cattle trade in the 1830s and 1840s, and which followed the already strong grain market, had carried the changes into even the more remote straths. The overall impact built up into a sweeping transformation of the rural landscape.

The visual changes, which included new roads and bridges, new farm buildings and layouts, an expansion of arable ground and the enclosure of fields, and new practises in the management of crops and livestock, were accompanied by a major upheaval of the rural population. The consolidation of farms into new larger units involved the engrossment of smaller tenant holdings and loss of subtenancies. Some of these people remained locally to supply the skills and labour needed by Improvement and amongst these were those who secured leases as colonising crofters around the margins of the improved farms. However, the net effect of these changes was a sharp acceleration in the drift away from the land. The growing rural population had already been losing people to the expanding cities and colonies for many decades, but these earlier emigrations had been mainly to remove the natural increases in the population. By the 1830s and 1840s, emigration had increased to the extent that it was depleting the rural communities

Fig 5.2   The Number of Parish Heritors in Aberdeenshire,
1791, 1843, 1872

Districts	Number of parishes	Total number of parish heritors			Average number of heritors per parish		
		1791	1843	1872	1791	1843	1872
1. Deeside & Alford	23	116	109	114	5.0	4.7	5.0
2. Huntly & Garioch	22	88	92	111	4.0	4.2	5.0
3. Turriff, Ellon & Deer	26	153	167	206	5.9	6.4	7.9
4. Aberdeen	11	90	113	118	8.2	10.3	10.7
Aberdeenshire	82	447	481	549	5.5	5.9	6.7

themselves. The trend towards the complete disappearance of subtenancies was rapidly concluded in the 1840s. A proposed new poor law
had threatened to increase the landowners' responsibilities for people
living on their estates and, as a result, wholesale evictions were
reported from throughout Aberdeenshire.

The 1830s and 1840s were a major watershed in the history of the
British countryside, as during these decades the overall balance tipped
from rural to urban. In areas like Aberdeenshire, the impact of the
landuse changes on the rural population was reinforced by the collapse
of essential income sources, like hand-knitting and illicit distilling.
After these decades, the population figures for most parishes went into
a sharp and long decline. The rural population of Aberdeenshire was,
with the exception of the lairds, ministers and dominies, a tenant
population and all the farms were tenanted except the lairds' home
farms. There was a stark contrast between the upheaval and deprivations
amongst this rural population and the constancy in the pattern of
landownership and composition of landowners.

The profitability of landownership continued to improve during the
19th century until the 1870s. Rents, for example, which had doubled
again between 1794 and 1814, continued to increase into the 1870s, as
did grain and livestock prices. There were hiccups in these trends such
as the repeal of the Corn Laws in 1846 and the Rhinderpest outbreak
of 1865, but these were short-lived setbacks. It was a financial climate
where no landowners could afford to ignore the improvement of their
estate and none wished to, as money could be borrowed at 6½% and

recouped from the tenants at 8%. Both the landlords and the new generation of capitalistic tenants strove to make the most of the land, the one from the rents they could obtain and the other from the market prices, both for profit. However, this unity of interests was limited, even in the great period of prosperous farming between 1850 and 1870 and even between the landlords and the main capitalistic tenants, like Aberdeenshire's famous cattle breeder William McCombie. The three most prominent contentions between these groups at this time were game, compensation and hypothec. The first was concerned with the damage done to the tenants' crops by animals reserved for the lairds' sport and the second with the lack of any recompense to a tenant for unexhausted improvements at the end of a tenancy. The third, the landlords' 'hypothec in the soil' was an old Scots law which gave them the right to claim any debts from the estate of a deceased tenant or any who had fallen into arrears, in preference to virtually all other creditors except the Crown.

The early 1870s were the high point of Victorian prosperity for landowners and reflected the hundred stable and profitable years since the 1770s. Even relatively small estates boasted rich mansions and the landowners often indulged in conspicuous consumption. Compared with their fathers and grandfathers, many landowners were divorced from the land. They needed to commit capital to it, but the land was not necessarily a business they needed to understand or with which they needed to be directly involved. Land was for prestige, for sport and for income and not for working, as the managers and tenants saw to that. Landowners were on the crest of a wave, reaping the dividends of earlier improvements and drawing an increment they themselves had not earned. This is not to say the landowners did not care for the land, but their separation from it was the downfall of many when the wave broke in the late 1870s and 1880s. The profits from the land were then no longer sufficient to keep them in the manner to which they had become accustomed.

The pattern of landownership in Aberdeenshire and all of Scotland's counties at the peak of Victorian prosperity in the early 1870s was recorded by the only government survey that there has ever been of landownership in Britain. Superficially, the results suggest a marked change in the pattern. However, a closer examination shows that the change was only a big increase in the number of extremely small landowners and that the underlying estate structure had continued remarkably unaltered.

The 1872 survey records 4489 landowners for Aberdeenshire.

Fig 5.3   Landownership Valuation Classes, Aberdeenshire 1872*

Valuation (££s)	Number of owners in class	Valuation for class (££s)	Percentage of total valuation
2-5	2	9	0.001
5-10	12	91	0.012
10-20	46	713	0.092
20-50	210	6,007	0.78
50-100	138	9,737	1.27
100-200	107	15,153	1.97
200-50	118	36,232	4.71
500-1,000	75	54,018	7.03
1,000-2,000	71	99,378	12.93
2,000-5,000	53	166,329	21.64
5,000-10,000	27	191,186	24.87
10,000-20,000	7	92,672	12.05
over 20,000	3	97,366	12.66
Total	869	768,791	100%

* Excluding owners of less than 1 acre

However, 3620 of these had less than one acre each and owned only 1258 acres in total, or less than 0.1% of Aberdeenshire. These numerous small owners were concentrated into the towns and villages of the county and included both house owners and the premises of a wide range of merchants, firms and institutions. Excluding these smallest owners, there were 869 owners with more than one acre each, consisting of 784 private owners and 85 owners in the other categories of premises.

Fig 5.3 records the distribution of Aberdeenshire's valuation between these 869 owners. This shows that the great majority were very small owners. For example, nearly half (408) had valuations less than £100 (Sterling), the level that was required then to qualify as a parish heritor, and three quarters (650) owned less than 10% of the county's assessed valuation between them. Above these small owners, the concentrated pattern of large-scale ownership still survived.

A comparison of the distributions of the county's valuation between landowners in 1771 and 1872 suggests a degree of dilution in the pattern of landownership. For example, 50% of the assessed valuation

*Fig 5.4   Ownership of Aberdeenshire by Percentage Valuation and
Number of Owners (1771 and 1872)*

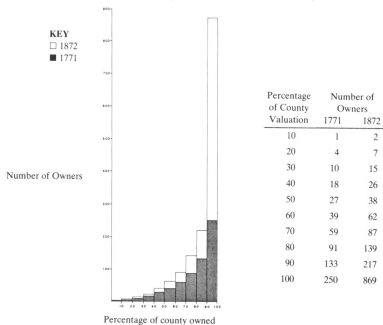

KEY
□ 1872
■ 1771

Number of Owners

Percentage of county owned

Percentage of County Valuation	Number of Owners 1771	1872
10	1	2
20	4	7
30	10	15
40	18	26
50	27	38
60	39	62
70	59	87
80	91	139
90	133	217
100	250	869

was held by 27 owners in 1771 and 38 owners in 1872 (Fig 5.4).
However, even this relatively small degree of change is misleading, as
it mainly results from the relatively higher valuations of smaller landholdings, and not from any significant loss in the extent of the county
held by the larger landowners.

The 1872 survey also recorded the acreage held by each landowner
and this gives a clearer picture of the pattern of landownership both in
Aberdeenshire and Scotland as a whole (Fig 5.5). Out of the 869
owners with more than one acre, only 461 had lands worth £100 or
more and so made up Aberdeenshire's 549 parish heritors. However,
these 461 owners still included many small owners. Only 339 owners in
the county had 100 acres or more each and these landowners held over
99% of Aberdeenshire between them. Thus, out of the 4489 landowners
recorded for Aberdeenshire in 1872, 4150 owned less than 1% of
Aberdeenshire's 1¼ million acres between them.

The pattern of landownership amongst these 339 owners with 99%
of Aberdeenshire's land between them, was itself very concentrated.

Fig 5.5
Landownership Acreage Classes
Aberdeenshire and Scotland 1872

SIZE (Acres)	ABERDEENSHIRE*			SCOTLAND		
	Number of owners	Acreage in size class	Percentage of total acreage	Number of owners	Acreage in size class	Percentage of total acreage
Under 1 acre	6,492	2,274	0.2	113,006	28,177	0.1
1-10	421	1,333	0.1	9,471	29,327	0.1
10-50	182	3,822	0.3	3,469	77,619	0.4
50-100	38	2,658	0.2	1,213	86,483	0.5
100-500	126	30,411	2.4	2,367	536,372	2.8
500-1000	58	42,037	3.4	826	582,741	3.1
1,000-2,000	60	87,466	7.0	591	835,242	4.4
2,000-5,000	46	158,214	12.6	587	1,843,378	9.7
5,000-10,000	25	179,083	14.3	250	1,726,869	9.1
10,000-20,000	14	186,302	14.8	159	2,150,111	11.4
20,000-50,000	5	120,882	9.6	103	3,071,728	16.2
50,000-100,000	4	300,827	24.0	44	3,025,616	16.0
over 100,000	1	139,829	11.1	24	4,931,884	26.0
Unspecified Land	—	—	—	22	1,147	
Total	7,472	1,255,138	100%	132,131	18,946,694	100%

* Includes Aberdeen Burgh with a total area of 1,780 acres and 2,983 owners.
The largest owner in the burgh had 103 acres and only 3 others had more than 50 acres.

Over half of them had less than 1,000 acres each and together owned less than 6% of the county. This was the main size of bracket of landholding that had been increasing in number during the 19th century. By this time, the demand for small estates had spread to most parts of the county, encouraged by the improved roads and the new railways.

Above the 184 landowners with 100-999 acres, were 155 landowners with 1,000 acres or more each. These larger landowners held 93.4% of Aberdeenshire and it was really within their ranks that the pattern of landownership was determined. It was a pattern of progressively fewer and larger landowners, culminating in the single largest owner owning more than 10% of the whole county. This was the Earl of Fife with 139,829 acres. However, as with the other Great Landlords in 1872, this was only a part of the Earl's estates. The Earl of Fife held a total of 249,220 acres in Aberdeenshire, Banff and Moray. Similarly, the Duke of Richmond and Gordon, who only had 69,660 acres in

Fig 5.6   Number of Landowners owning Aberdeenshire and Scotland
by Percentage Acreage 1872

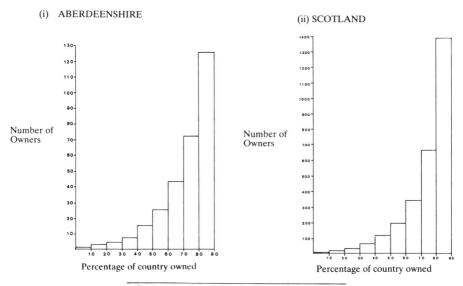

(i) ABERDEENSHIRE

(ii) SCOTLAND

Percentage	Number of Owners holding that extent	
of area	Aberdeenshire	Scotland
10	1	3
20	3	21
30	4	34
40	7	63
50	15	11.8
60	25	196
70	43	342
80	72	659
90	126	1380

Aberdeenshire, had 241,883 acres in total with his lands in Banff and
Moray. At least 90 of Aberdeenshire's top 155 landowners in 1872 had
lands outside Aberdeenshire, scattered across the rest of Britain and
Ireland. The gross annual value of their holdings in Aberdeenshire was
£488,962 and the value of their other lands not far short at £369,092.

A comparison between the statistics for the valuations and acreages
of estates in 1872, reflects the fact that smaller estates tended to have
relatively higher valuations. In 1872, 90% of Aberdeenshire's land
area was still held by 126 landowners, even though the number of

landowners sharing 90% of the county's valuation had increased from 133 to 217 since 1771. The distribution of the land between the landowners holding 90% of its area is illustrated for both Aberdeenshire and Scotland as a whole in Fig 5.6. The patterns for each were very similar, reflecting a pyramid of fewer and larger landowners. At the Scottish scale, for example, 75% of Scotland was owned by 580 individuals and 50% by just 118. A comparison with England, which also had its Great Landlords, brings out the nature of the Scottish pattern. In 1872, 58% of Scotland was owned by landowners with estates of 20,000 acres or more, while in England this size of owner held less than 7% of the country.

The pattern of largescale landownership in Scotland in 1872 was not uniform across the whole country. Fig 5.7 compares the Scottish counties on the basis of the percentage of each county owned by landowners with 1,000 acres or more. The figure of 93.4% for Aberdeenshire was similar to the average for all the counties of 92.8%. This high national average reflects the relatively small degree of variation across the whole of Scotland. However, the pattern that emerges is that larger landowners held their greatest extent in the Borders, the North-east and Highlands, with their least extent in the west and central belt. This was the same pattern as had existed 100 years before and during earlier centuries.

The composition of the main landowners had changed little in Scotland or Aberdeenshire since the 18th century. These large landowners were invariably from families with a long history as major landowners. Fig 5.8 lists the largest landowners in Aberdeenshire at 1872. Whether measured by acreage or valuation, broadly the same owners tend to come out on top. The limited changes during the 19th century are illustrated by the occurrence of 21 of the 25 top landowners in 1802 in the 1872 list. Even the four who do not appear in 1872, still held significant estates in Aberdeenshire: Skene of Dyce (8,992 acres), Elphinstone of Logie (5,524), Farquharson of Haughton (4,500), and Gordon of Buthlaw (1,124).

There were seven new entries in the 1872 lists compared to the list for 1802. Most of these were from traditional landowning families in Aberdeenshire. The Abercrombies were already baronets when they had acquired Forglen, an estate focussed in Banffshire, before the end of the 17th century. The Dingwall-Fordyces represented the joining of two landowning families by marriage. The Dingwalls had acquired Brucklay in the first decade of the 18th century by marriage to Irvines and the Fordyces had bought Culsh and Gask at the same period from

Fig 5.7   Landownership in Scotland 1872:
Owners with 1,000 acres or more by County
(excluding the Northern Isles)

County	Total area of county	Number of owners with 1,000 acres or more	Acreage held by these owners	Percentage of county held by them
Aberdeen	1,255,138	155	1,172,603	93.4
Angus	555,994	75	489,159	87.9
Argyll	2,030,948	146	2,005,521	98.7
Ayr	721,947	100	618,040	85.6
Banff	407,501	28	399,310	98.0
Berwick	292,049	51	245,322	84.0
Bute	138,972	4	136,954	98.5
Caithness	471,763	29	469,536	99.5
Clackmannan	30,180	7	24,761	82.0
Dumbarton	153,736	23	120,756	78.5
Dumfries	676,971	74	595,609	88.0
East Lothian	171,739	35	149,215	86.9
Fife	304,363	74	193,914	63.7
Inverness	2,589,408	89	2,576,261	99.5
Kirkcudbright	571,950	92	500,749	87.6
Kincardine	244,585	41	219,818	89.9
Kinross	44,888	8	11,963	26.7
Lanark	557,919	87	412,675	74.0
Midlothian	231,742	50	172,586	74.5
Moray	303,168	27	292,633	96.5
Nairn	120,765	11	116,646	96.6
Peebles	232,410	40	222,702	95.8
Perth	1,612,840	158	1,510,228	93.6
Renfrew	155,321	25	155,979	74.7
Ross & Cromarty	1,989,888	69	1,595,997	80.2
Roxburgh	423,463	67	381,559	90.1
Selkirk	161,815	28	154,183	92.3
Stirling	284,751	42	209,708	73.6
Sutherland	1,299,253	11	1,294,785	99.7
West Lothian	75,785	17	46,914	61.9
Wigton	309,087	32	296,863	96.0
Totals	18,946,694	1,758	17,584,828	Average 92.8

Fig 5.8   Top 25 Landowners by Acreage and Valuation
in Aberdeenshire 1872

(i)   BY ACREAGE

	Acres
1. Earl of Fife	139,829
2. James Farquharson of Invercauld	87,745
3. Marquis of Huntly	80,000
4. Duke of Richmond and Gordon	69,660
5. Earl of Aberdeen	63,422
6. Sir Charles Forbes of Newe	29,238
7. H.M. The Queen	25,350
8. Sir James McKenzie of Glenmuick	25,000
9. Arthur Dingwall-Fordyce of Brucklay	20,899
10. John Gordon of Cluny	20,395
11. Earl of Kintore	17,021
12. Francis Farquharson of Finzean	16,809
13. Hugh Gordon Lumsden of Clova & Auchindoir	15,499
14. General John Forbes of Inveranan	15,366
15. Sir Archibald Grant of Monymusk	14,881
16. Lord Forbes	13,621
17. Carlos Pedro Gordon of Wardhouse & Kildrummy	13,427
18. Colonel Alex Leith-Hay of Rannes	12,546
19. George Ferguson of Pitfour	12,305
20. Alex Gordon of Fyvie	11,700
21. Garden Duff of Hatton	11,576
22. Trustees of late George Baird of Strichen	11,248
23. Alex Morrison of Bognie	10,251
24. Lord Saltoun	10,082
25. Sir William Forbes of Craigievar	9,347

Irvines. In 1744, the Dingwall laird, who worked as a Writer of the Signet in Edinburgh, married the Fordyce heiress. The Bannermans had acquired Crimonmogate in the first half of the 18th century. The estate had passed through debt into the hands of Alex Milne, a merchant in Aberdeen. His daughter married the Provost of Aberdeen, Patrick Bannerman, to whom the estate passed. The Earls of Crawford and Balcarres were Lindsays, who had received an earldom in the 17th century. Although they acquired their main landholding in Aberdeenshire in the early 19th century, they had had landowning associations in the North-east since at least the 16th century.

This meant that only three of the landowners in the 1872 lists had joined the ranks of Aberdeenshire's landowners during the 19th century. These were: Queen Victoria, who had acquired Balmoral from the Earl of Fife in 1852; Sir James McKenzie, the son of an Aberdeen silk mercer, who had made his money abroad and bought

(ii) BY VALUATION

££s Sterling

1. Duke of Richmond and Gordon	79,683	
2. Earl of Fife	72,563	
3. Earl of Aberdeen	44,112	
4. Earl of Crawford and Balcarres	39,252	(8855)*
5. Sir Reginald Cathcart-Gordon of Cluny	38,188	
6. Lord Clinton (Forbes)	32,613	
7. Earl of Kintore	29,551	
8. H.M. The Queen	27,995	
9. George Baird of Strichen	23,199	
10. George Ferguson of Pitfour	19,938	
11. Marquis of Huntly	19,860	
12. Charles Leslie of Balquhain	18,822	(8940)*
13. Arthur Dingwall-Fordyce of Brucklay	14,058	
14. James Farquharson of Invercauld	12,974	
15. Sir Robert Abercromby of Forglen, Turriff	12,395	(1942)*
16. Lord Saltoun	11,929	
17. Lachlan Gordon-Duff of Drummuir, Keith	10,447	(4328)*
18. Alexander Gordon of Fyvie	10,111	
19. Robert W. Duff of Fetteresso	9,803	(1588)*
20. Garden Duff of Hatton	9,661	
21. Earl of Erroll (Slains)	9,599	(4249)*
22. John Udny of Udny	9,041	(9225)*
23. Sir William Forbes of Craigievar	8,539	
24. Sir Alexander Bannerman of Elsick & Crimonmogate	8,446	(7660)*
25. Mrs Baird of Cambusdoon (Auchmedden)	8,043	(5976)*

*Acreage if not listed in (i)

Glenmuick estate from Farquharson of Invercauld: George Baird, an Ayrshire businessman, who had bought Strichen from the Frasers in 1855, when they sold it to pay off debts on their main family estates in Inverness-shire.

This pattern of longstanding owners and scarcely any incomers was not restricted to just the top thirty or so landowners. It spread throughout the ranks of all the landowners with 1,000 acres or more. Considering just the 106 owners with lands valued at £1,500 per annum and more, who owned more than 75% of Aberdeenshire, only twelve had acquired their estates in the previous fifty years. Eighty-nine of these 106 owners had been in their estates since the 18th century and at least 79 of them had held their lands since before 1750.

The very active land market during the 19th century, with estates being bought and sold, tended to create the impression of new landowners or incomers taking over the county. However, many of the sales were of the same properties. This reflected the strong tendency

71

for estates to be sold more rapidly by incomers, than estates were sold by traditional owners. There was therefore limited penetration of the pattern of landownership by incomers and by 1872, their share of the county was still only of the order of 15-25%. Numerically, by far the greatest concentrations of incomers were in the parishes around Aberdeen and in parts of East Aberdeenshire. However, the creation of a small number of new estates in Deeside accounted for about a quarter of the incomers' share of the county's acreage.

These new Deeside estates came out of the lands of the valley's traditional large landowners, but were typically formed from peripheral areas that had already been exchanged, albeit slowly, between these big landowners. The east side of Glenmuick had been held by the Huntlys for 400 years when it was sold to the Farquharsons of Invercauld in 1749, who then sold it to Sir James McKenzie a century later. Balmoral had been bought from Invercauld by the Earl of Fife in 1798 before it was sold to the Queen in 1852. The Queen added Birkhall in 1855 for the Prince of Wales. This was a portion of west Glenmuick that had been owned previously by the Gordons of Abergeldie for nearly 400 years. In 1878, the Queen also added Ballochbuie to safeguard the ancient pinewood there from felling. She bought it from the Farquharsons of Invercauld, who themselves had obtained it from the Earls of Fife in 1782. Another newly created estate in mid-Deeside was Corrachee. This had been Farquharson land and then gone to the Huntlys, out of whose estates it was sold to James Farquharson in 1842, when he returned wealthy from East India service. The break-up of the 16th century Gordon of Blelack estate during the nineteenth century also resulted in new small estates in mid-Deeside, most prominently Tillypronie, which was bought in 1855 by Sir James Clarke, the Queen's physician.

Large landowners like the Earls of Fife, the Farquharsons of Invercauld and the Marquis of Huntly, might occasionally buy and sell lands, with some areas being traded between them over the centuries as their fortunes varied. However, all landowners had strong reasons for not selling land. Apart from the potential income it offered in the profitable decades before the 1870s, landownership still conferred many other social, political and economic advantages. The loss of land was synonymous with failure in a fuller sense than just financial. As in all previous centuries, the landowners' imperative was the continued possession of their estates. This attachment to the land was greatest in the traditional landowning families and they still had over 75% of Aberdeenshire in 1872.

The successful survival of the century between 1771-1872 by such a high proportion of these old landowning families was not simply due to the favourable economic climate or good estate management. The landowners' hold on their estates was buttressed both by the Scots laws of property and by a range of legal and financial arrangements to guard against any eventuality. As Sir John Sinclair, the authority of his day on rural Scotland had commented in 1814, "In no country in Europe are the rights of proprietors so well defined and so carefully protected".

The laws of entail and the establishment of trusts were two of the common strategies that allowed families to retain lands that would otherwise have needed to be sold. The laws of entail dated from 1685 and still remain in force, though the creation of new entails has been prohibited since 1914. The great majority of Aberdeenshire's largest 100 estates during the 19th century were entailed. This meant, for example, the lands could not be claimed by creditors in the event of financial failure. These entailment bonds were sometimes broken, perhaps in as many as half the cases where they were tested. However, this was often achieved to suit the purposes of the family involved, as entailed land could be an obstacle to a landowner's own plans and an Act of 1770 had relaxed the conditions of entails in the interests of Improvement.

Many important landowners still ran into debt in the first three quarters of the nineteenth century and it was in these cases that entailment allowed the storm to be weathered into the next generation. For example, with the Farquharsons of Finzean, Archibald Farquharson, the laird in the early 19th century, went bankrupt in the 1840s. He had spent extravagant sums on legal battles and on his own indulgent lifestyle. The legal battles had been mainly against the Earl of Aboyne, whose lands marched with Finzean's in several parishes and who also went bankrupt in the 1840s. Archibald Farquharson was also very partial to gambling and, after his marriage to the Russell heiress of the neighbouring Feughside estate of Blackhall, he had his own racecourse built there.

When Archibald Farquharson became bankrupt, Blackhall was the only land lost. The other 16,000 acres of his estate, including the home lands of Finzean and extensive portions of Lumphanan and Migvie parishes, were entailed. Therefore the Farquharson ownership of them continued secure and the Farquharsons of Finzean were still the 12th biggest landowners in the county in 1872. The bankruptcy did, however, have a profound impact on the well-being and development of the communities living on these Finzean lands. The creditors were able to claim what they could and, for example, it was reported that not one timber tree bigger than a walking stick was left standing anywhere on the Finzean lands. Further, it was many years before Archibald's successors secured loans to carry out improvements on the estate, so that at the height of the Improvement era, the Finzean lands were languishing in relative stagnation. Thus, it was localities that bore the brunt of a bankruptcy and not necessarily the acreage of the bankrupt owner's estate. Similarly, the assets of a locality and possible estate investment were the first casualties of a landowner's financial difficulties, even when these did not go the full length of bankruptcy.

The other strategy to safeguard landowners' lands was the establishment of trusts. These could be formed to look after entailed estates when the owner was bankrupt, but they were also important in maintaining estates against other non-financial threats. There was a range of circumstances where landowners might not be able to continue in direct possession of their estates and trusts were formed to prevent the sale of the lands. These circumstances principally included minority (under age), madness or imprisonment. The importance of these trust arrangements is illustrated by the fact that virtually every main Aberdeenshire estate was managed by a trust at some stage between 1670-1870. Initially there were sometimes difficulties with trustees milking the lands under their control for their own benefit as, for example, on the Aboyne lands in the early 18th century. However, by the nineteenth century, trusts were more sophisticated and secure arrangements.

These legal and financial mechanisms were most common over the larger estates of the traditional landowning families, while the sales of land were most frequent amongst the incomers on the smaller estates. Both groups however, were usually not just dependent on the incomes from their estates. Many of the traditional families received major injections of capital and interest from the same sources as were providing incomers with their new wealth. The sons of the traditional families were, for example, equally involved in the expansion and development of the Empire, often obtaining a preferential start because of their background. India was the classic source of wealth where many landowning families, new and old, made fortunes. The Nicols, for example, who bought the three adjacent Aberdeenshire estates of Ballogie, Balnacraig and Midstrath in the 1850s and 1860s, had been subtenants during the 18th century and subsequently had success in India with a family company, Wm. Nicol and Co., in Bombay.

A conspicuous example of an old landowning family's success in India was the Forbes family of Newe. They had owned Newe since at least the 16th century and in the mid 18th century it passed by collateral descent to John Forbes. He had spent his youth in India and founded the merchant banking firm of House of Forbes in Bombay, and in the late 18th century used his wealth to start improving Newe. In the early 19th century, he was succeeded by his nephew Charles Forbes, who was created first Baronet of Newe in 1823. Charles Forbes had worked in the House of Forbes in Bombay until 1811 and then applied his Indian wealth to Newe. He added Skellater and Corgarff estates from other Forbes landowners, built a new Castle Newe, which also involved re-routing the Donside road across the river, and undertook sweeping improvements on his estates. The design of the new castle, including the road re-alignment, were to be remarkably paralleled by Queen Victoria half a century later, though her twelve mile stretch of Deeside was modest compared with the thirty miles of Donside embraced within Newe.

The prosperity and confidence that landowning had acquired by the middle years of Victoria's reign, were abruptly reduced during the 1870s and 1880s. A sharp decrease in profits was accompanied by an upsurge in rural unrest. The economic decline was not a brief downturn, as had occurred on several occasions earlier in the century. It was the end of an era and the whole British economy felt its effects. It was due to a combination of events that undermined the profitability of home produced goods and foods. The end of the Franco-Prussian war in 1871, meant that British manufacturers faced new competition at home and abroad. The end of the American Civil War resulted in the arrival of cheap grain and this was accentuated by a run of bad harvests through the 1870s. Then, in the 1880s, the livestock sector, which had missed the worst of the initial onslaught, was undercut by the arrival of cheap meat from Australasia and South America, which had been made possible by the development of refridgeration.

The rural discontent, which had been gathering strength during the times of plenty came to a head in the deteriorating economic climate. The 1872 survey of landownership had itself been a symptom of mounting pressure. The Prime Minister, Lord Derby, had commissioned the survey to disprove allegations that the landownership of the whole of Britain was dominated by only 30,000 people. The survey revealed that even the allegations had been too generous and that, in fact, four-fifths of the whole country were held by only 7000 individuals.

The Scottish Farms Alliance (S.F.A.) was the main organisation in

Scotland pushing for land reform. The S.F.A. obtained 80% of its funds from Aberdeenshire, which was a focus for land agitation at that time. The demands being made covered a wide range of issues including the abolition of hypothec, entails and primogeniture, the reform of the game laws, the establishment of the tenants' right of compensation, as well as security and heritable tenure under a judicial rent controlled by a land court. By 1881, with the Irish Land Act fresh on the statute books, the S.F.A. had become firmly linked with Gladstone and his Liberal Party and, in the end, this was to be the movement's undoing.

Land agitation in Aberdeenshire, as elsewhere in Scotland, reached its peak in 1886. Some demands had already been achieved, for example, over hypothec and the Game Laws and, with the 1883 Agricultural Holdings Act (Scotland), the tenants' right to compensation. These satisfied some of the S.F.A.'s supporters and the S.F.A. changed its name to the Scottish Land Reform Alliance (S.L.R.A.) to try and retain its mass membership. Optimism for reform continued with the strong possibility that the North-east would be included in the Crofters Holdings Act sponsored by the Liberal government. The government's reasons for choosing just the seven 'crofting counties' (the small average size of holdings, the existence of Gaelic and historical evidence of common grazings) were all shown to be equally the case for the North-east counties. Finally, thwarted at trying to find a rational basis for limiting it to the 'crofting counties', the Government simply opted for those counties visited by the Napier Commission and the amendment to include the North-east was defeated by 126-87 votes.

1886 was a turning point for the S.L.R.A.'s objectives. Gladstone's government collapsed over Home Rule for Ireland and the concentration on Home Rule over the next decades took radical land reform off the British political agenda. The radical movement was also compromised by its leaders. The S.L.R.A.'s parliamentary spokesmen were the Liberals Dr Robert Farquharson and J.W. Barclay. Dr Farquharson was the laird of Finzean, one of Aberdeenshire's biggest estates, and Barclay, who was to become the laird of Glenbuchat, was a tenant on Finzean estate. Barclay had originally been an Aberdeen merchant, before becoming a large-scale capitalist farmer through a lease on Auchlossan. It was hardly surprising that these two representatives did not pursue the case against landlord oppression as vigorously as the mass of their supporters wanted.

The economic and political events of the 1870s and 1880s were an important watershed in the development of landownership in Scotland. However, they had little immediate effect on the pattern of landowner-ship and composition of landowners during the last decades of the nineteenth' century. The loss of political momentum by the rural population meant that the economic decline had the most important consequences. The fall in the profitability of agriculture and the improved terms for tenants tended to be felt hardest on the smaller estates. Many of these in Aberdeenshire were factored by lawyers in Aberdeen and had been the estates keenest at raising their rents, because more of these owners relied on a narrower estate income. The larger estates had a broader base and their owners were more likely to have outside sources of income. Sport in particular remained increasingly profitable as a landuse, especially deer stalking. In the highlands of Aberdeenshire, this did not lead to a marked increase in the number of deer forests, as it did in the rest of the Highlands. All Aberdeenshire's main deer forests had been established between 1770-1870 and were prominent amongst Scotland's earliest deer forests. The change after the 1870s was more focused on an increased economic exploitation of sport, exemplified by expensive leases to wealthy industrial or foreign shooting tenants.

The Royal estates of Balmoral and Birkhall were a classic example of a sporting estate and the 10,000 acre estate of Abergeldie was also leased to add to the sporting potential available to the Royal family and their guests. The enthusiasm of Victoria and Albert for their Highland estate, paradoxically set in the heart of the Jacobite country of the 1715 and 1745 risings, was also an important influence on maintaining and encouraging the fashion amongst the wealthy for a Scottish estate. Shooting tenants were prepared to pay rich rents and there was never a shortage of incomers prepared to buy their way in and pay for the privilege of joining the landed class. The decline in profitability of estates as a whole simply raised the threshold, by making a continuing outside income more necessary. However, land had always had a market value above its productive potential.

The existing landowners faced increasing financial difficulties during the last decades of the 19th century, with estates no longer providing the revenue to keep the owners in the manner to which they had been long accustomed. However, the recession had little effect on the pattern of landownership with most of the sales that occurred merely allowing more outside wealth to buy in. In Aberdeenshire, the main casualty of the period was the Marquis of Huntly, whose family fell into financial difficulty once more. In 1869, he had married Amy, elder daughter of an autocratic Manchester banking tycoon, Sir William Cunliffe Brooks. In 1870, Sir William leased Glen Tanar from the Marquis and then, in 1888, he bought Aboyne Castle and estate, adding to this the purchase of Glen Tanar in the early 1890s. In 1897, the Marquis' Birse estate was sold to Robert Heaven, who was the American ambassador in London. Sir William Cunliffe Brooks invested large sums into the Marquis' former estates, employing a work force of 250 and including some extravagant gestures that matched his eccentric character. Sir William died in 1900 and his estates were sold by his grandson to an Aberdeen merchant, who promptly resold them to Sir C.M. Barclay Harvey, who in turn resold the Castle and grounds back to the Marquis of Huntly, so that their connection was not severed totally.

Most of the limited number of sales during this period were of small estates. One or two middling estates were sold more profitably as two or three smaller estates, but there was no conspicuous move towards a 'break-up' of estates. The traditional families held on and cut back on their expenditure. The condition of tenant farms and houses was allowed to slide and little investment went into other estate responsibilities, such as forestry. Some larger estates just sold off a small portion of their domains to ease their situation. For example, the Earl of Aberdeen sold his Ellon lands in 1889 and the Earl of Fife sold Glenbuchat a few years after. In 1894, estate duty was introduced and was an extra burden on the larger landowners. This, and the continuing recession, brought many estates to the brink of survival by the end of the century. However, in 1899/1900, the earlier 19th century pattern of landownership in Aberdeenshire was still substantially intact. More sales were talked of than occurred, as landowners warned of the impending break-up of their estates. The demise of one or two lent weight to these words but, as with the scare of penetration by incomers earlier in the century, the late 19th century conveyed more impression of a reduction in landownership than actually occurred.

The 19th century had seen the pattern of landownership in Aberdeenshire, and Scotland as a whole, pass a peak of concentration. The trend was first reversed within the ranks of the small landowners and then, towards the end of the century, fragmentation started to spread up the scale of ownership. However, by the end of the century, the final years of Queen Victoria's reign, economic change and political reform had had little impact on the overall pattern of landownership. The 1,500 largest landowners in Scotland had held over

90% of the country in 1872 and this had only dropped a percentage point or two 30 years later.

The longstanding pattern of concentrated largescale landownership in Scotland reached the 20th century more or less intact. The greatest change had been in the confidence and prosperity of the owners, who had had both their profits and political influence reduced.

Chapter 6

The 20th Century

There have been some important changes in the pattern of
landownership in Scotland during the 20th century. These changes
have involved three main elements: a reduction in the area held by the
larger estates, including the wholesale division and sale of some of the
largest; an increase in the number of small owners, particularly of
owner-occupied farms and houses; a major expansion in the extent of
land owned by the state and public agencies.

These changes have occurred at different rates during different
periods of this century and have been more extensive in some parts of
the country than others. Some of the changes like the break-up of
some major estates have been very conspicuous and this has tended to
create the impression that the overall pattern of landownership in
Scotland has been fundamentally altered during the last 100 years.
However, the effect of all the changes has been less than is sometimes
suggested and the longstanding pattern of large-scale estates continues
to be clearly recognisable.

An initial context within which to measure the changes during the
20th century is provided by a comparison between the estate structure
in 1872 and 1970. 1872 was the height of prosperity and confidence in
Victorian landownership and 1970 is the most recent date for which
comprehensive statistics are available. During this period, the limited
reduction in the number of estates has been most marked amongst the
largest estates. The number of estates of 20,000 acres or more fell from
171 to 121, while the number of estates of 5,000 acres or more showed
a smaller reduction from 576 to 546 and the number of estates of 1,000
acres or more only changed from 1,758, to 1,723.

This comparison indicates that the traditional estate structure survived with a fair degree of constancy during the period 1872 to 1970. However, it also indicates that the resilience of this underlying pattern has been accompanied by a reduction in the extent of Scotland held within each size category of estate. For example, the average proportion of Scotland's counties held in estates of 1,000 acres or more fell from 92.8% in 1872 to 62.8% in 1970. The surviving pattern of estates therefore now covers 30% less of the country and the growth of small owners and state ownership during this century can be viewed as occurring within this 30%.

The overall changes in Aberdeenshire conform closely to those in the wider Scottish pattern. For example, there were 155 estates of 1,000 acres or more in 1872 and still 139 of that size in 1970, while their share of Aberdeenshire fell by 29.8%. This reduction had already been underway before the end of the 19th century. The market demand for smaller properties had encouraged some reduction by the mid 19th century. The economic recession from the 1870s onwards then forced an increasing number of sales where the land was sold into smaller units than under the previous ownership. The most conspicuous casualty in Aberdeenshire during the late 19th century had been the county's third largest landowner, the Marquis of Huntly. His 80,000 acre estate on Deeside was sold into three separate main estates: Glen Tanar, Aboyne and Dinnet, and Birse of approximately 34,000, 27,000 and 14,000 acres respectively.

During the first decades of the 20th century, landowners' incomes from their estates had continued to decline. Fig 6.1, based on Income Tax returns, shows that land-derived income fell by over a quarter between the mid 1870s and 1910. At the same time, landowners were also having to cope with a number of new taxes. In 1907, for example, an unearned income surcharge payable on rents was added to the estate duty that had been introduced in 1894. This surcharge on rents was particularly significant in Aberdeenshire, given the county's importance in Scottish agriculture at the time, both in terms of the number of farms and their total rental (Fig 6.2).

This deteriorating economic situation resulted in an increasing number of land sales. The gradual reduction of the fifth largest estate in Aberdeenshire, Newe (29,000 acres), had started in 1900 with three portions being sold off separately: Candacraig, Deskry and Delnadamph. Then, in 1908, Edinglassie was sold and, in 1911, part of Newe itself. The final sale of Newe Castle and the last of the lands took place in 1924. Several of the county's other main landowners were also selling off parts of their estates. The Duke (formerly Earl) of Fife, for

Fig 6.1   Gross income derived from the ownership of land as returned
under Schedule A of the Income Tax. Scotland
1870-71 and 1876-1910

	£		£
1870-71	7,301,182	1893-94	6,251,898
1876-77	7,689,717	1894-95	6,193,310
1877-78	7,666,090	1895-96	6,147,882
1878-79	7,667,629	1896-97	6,100,326
1879-80	7,769,303	1897-98	6,045,378
1880-81	7,711,895	1898-99	5,967,345
1881-82	7,648,589	1899-00	5,956,530
1882-83	7,573,251	1900-01	5,943,692
1883-84	7,505,321	1901-02	5,911,836
1884-85	7,461,957	1902-03	5,883,487
1885-86	7,320,599	1903-04	5,852,773
1886-87	7,099,580	1904-05	5,838,394
1887-88	6,824,100	1905-06	5,821,080
1888-89	6,539,762	1906-07	5,811,229
1889-90	6,416,507	1907-08	5,801,209
1890-91	6,374,863	1908-09	5,772,165
1891-92	6,318,581	1909-10	5,775,705
1892-93	6,291,119	1910-1911	5,757,167

example, continued to sell outlying portions of his lands, away from his main estate at Mar. He had sold the parish of Glenbuchat as a unit in the late 19th century and in 1905, he sold Glass parish (12,590 acres), dividing it into four separate estates.

Sales which involved the reduction or break-up of estates continued during the First World War. Two significant examples were the estates of the Earl of Kintore in 1914 and of Gordon of Ellon in 1919. These examples both illustrated the important new trend that was emerging — the purchase by estate tenants of their own holdings. The Earl of Kintore's estate of over 17,000 acres completely dominated the ownership of the parishes of Inverurie, Kintore and Keithhall, and was sold direct to the sitting tenants. The estate of Ellon Castle, which included the town, was sold after the death of Arthur Gordon. The estate was put up for auction in lots at a public roup and similarly resulted in many purchases by the former tenants. This new trend resulted in a significant growth of owner-occupied farms in Aberdeen-shire. The number increased from 438 in 1912 to 670 in 1920. However, this was only 6.3% of all farms and their combined acreage was still equally small at 53,000 acres.

The income from agriculture, which had been artificially high during

*Fig 6.2   Total number of farms in each county of Scotland
with gross rental, 1906*

County	No.	Rental			
Aberdeen	12,493	583,823	Lanark	3,568	329,645
Argyll	3,730	173,917	Linlithgow	681	68,382
Ayr	3,212	419,141	Midlothian	616	192,851
Banff	3,339	130,465	Nairn	379	22,211
Berwick	1,109	209,111	Orkney	3,387	48,447
Bute	732	28,158	Peebles	354	57,408
Caithness	3,235	68,295	Perth	5,380	416,890
Clackmannan	296	19,441	Renfrew	1,173	133,711
Dumbarton	853	63,811	Ross and Cromarty	7,790	122,405
Dumfries	3,415	304,964	Roxburgh	1,636	221,714
Elgin or Moray	1,691	91,519	Selkirk	329	39,979
Fife	3,652	300,728	Shetland	3,782	22,685
Forfar	3,160	310,902	Stirling	2,017	148,864
Haddington	878	169,957	Sutherland	3,105	31,394
Inverness	7,359	121,659	Wigtown	1,482	146,172
Kincardine	1,887	131,492	Total of Scotland	89,065	5,365,474
Kinross	359	32,125			
Kirkcudbright	1,956	203,208			

the 1st World War, had slumped back to a very depressed state by 1921 and this continued during the prolonged depression of the 1920s until the mid 1930s. The whole period involved a very conspicuous break-up of estates, particularly after the substantial increase in estate duty from 1925. Many of the sales were to the sitting tenants and the number of owner-occupied farms in Aberdeenshire increased from 670 to 2,588 between 1920 and 1930. Their combined acreage rose to 188,000 acres or 23% of the agricultural land in the county and 15% of the total land area. It was a trend that was occurring throughout Scotland. In 1914, 11% of Scottish farmland had been owner-occupied. By 1929, the figure was 29%, and in the following year it went up to 30.4%. The increase in Aberdeenshire during that year of 8.2% in the number of owner-occupiers, and the switch of 12,125 acres to owner occupation, where the largest changes in any county. In the 1930s, the owner-occupation of agricultural land continued to increase, but at a much slower rate than during the 1920s (Fig 6.3).

Several well-known Aberdeenshire estates were divided up and sold in the 1920s, including Leith Hall (12,500 acres) in the early 1920s and Strichen (11,500 acres) in 1925. Many other smaller estates were also broken up after the increase in estate duty in 1925. However, the largest increases in owner-occupation came from sales on the estates of

Fig 6.3   Owner-Occupation of Farms
Aberdeenshire and Scotland 1912-1940

| | | ABERDEENSHIRE | | | | SCOTLAND | |
Year	Total number of farms	Number owner-occupied	Percentage owner-occupied	Acreage owner-occupied	% of total agricultural acreage	% Farms owner-occupied	% agricultural acreage owner occupied
1912	10952	438	4	—	—	6.7	9.8
1920	10660	670	6.3	53,663	6.5	8.2	12.8
1930	10307	2588	25.1	188,090	23.0	21.2	30.4
1940	9859	3091	31.4	210,534	24.3	23.6	31.3

the Earl of Aberdeen and the Duke of Richmond and Gordon. They were two of the county's largest three landowners and both favoured the sale of farms to their tenants. The Earl of Aberdeen's estate had been gradually declining for many years between the sale of their Ellon lands in 1889 and their Deeside estate of Cromar in 1918. Taxation after 1925 accelerated this reduction with, for example, the sale to the tenants of 26,000 acres north of the Ythan near Methlick in the late twenties. The sales during this period still left the Earls of Aberdeen with the Haddo estate which has survived up to the present day. However the Duke of Richmond and Gordon's sales completely depleted his 70,000 acre estate in Aberdeenshire. The sales started in 1926 with the lands in Rhynie parish and were completed in 1936 with the last of the Duke's lands in Huntly and Gartly parishes. Most of the farms ended up with the tenants, either directly or through re-sale from the Forestry Commission (F.C.). The F.C. had acquired extensive tracts of the Duke's lands and established the Bin and Clashindarroch Forests out of their purchases. By 1934, the F.C. had already acquired land in Aberdeenshire for State Forests around Old Deer, Whitehaugh, Pitfichie, Kemnay, Kirkhill, Midmar, Glenmuick and Ballochbuie. The decline of the large estates was the right climate for the young Commission to acquire lands for afforestation and, by the mid 1930s, their acreage in Aberdeenshire was approaching 40,000.

The main exception to the sale of the Duke of Richmond and Gordon's farms to the tenants, were 10 farms near Huntly bought by Gordon of Troup. Eight of these were soon resold to Viscount Cowdray. The Cowdrays were a prominent reminder that not all estates were being broken up on sale, nor necessarily going to new or small owners. The Cowdrays were continuously expanding their estates in Aberdeenshire during the early decades of this century. They had first acquired the Earl of Crawford and Balcarres' 8,800 acre estate of Dunecht from a Mr Perry in 1905 and continued with other estate purchases, like Birse in 1911 and Castle Fraser in 1921. Other more modest examples of expanding landowners at this time included Sir Thomas Royden and his neighbours, the MacRoberts.

Sir Thomas Royden, like the Cowdrays, had extensive and successful outside business interests. He was, for example, a Director of Cunard, Shell, Phoenix and the Midland Bank. In 1925 he bought the estate of Blackmill and in 1934 Migvie. This later estate was purchased from the Farquharsons of Finzean on the death of Joseph Farquharson. Finzean's Lumphanan lands were also sold at the same time and the size of the estate reduced to half its 1872 acreage. This was a common trend during this period, when many old estates survived being completely broken up, by major reductions in their lands, allowing them to retain the traditional core areas of their estates intact. The MacRoberts, who had acquired Douneside in the late 19th century, added Cromar in 1918 and Melgum in 1929. The founder of this estate, Sir Alexander MacRobert, had been born in 1854 the son of an Aberdeenshire labourer and made his money in India, principally through steel.

The changes during the 1920s and early 1930s were a dramatic episode in the long history of Aberdeenshire's concentrated pattern of landownership. For many people, particularly those living in parishes that passed almost overnight into multiple ownership after centuries under a single Great Landlord, it appeared that the days of the large and traditional landowners were over. However, from the late 1930s, even though death duties were still a prominent cause of sales, the pressures eased on the surviving estates. Small estates continued to sell some farms to tenants and some larger estates to sell off portions. For example, Cluny estate sold Slains (2,500 acres) to McKenzie of Glenmuick in 1942 and the Grants of Monymusk sold 6,000 acres to the Forestry Commission in 1946. However, by the 1940s, the sale of farms and break-up of estates declined rapidly compared with the pace of events in the previous two decades. The 1920s and 1930s were a prominent period in the development of the pattern of landownership, yet the relatively limited overall changes for the whole period between 1872 and 1970, show that its impact was less than the prominence it has often been given.

In the post war period up until 1970, the overall tax burden on landowners continued to decline and at the same time, the government subsidies to agriculture and forestry increased rapidly. These changes strengthened the financial position of estates and also meant there was

Fig 6.4   Owner-Occupation of Farms
Aberdeenshire and Scotland 1940-1970

		ABERDEENSHIRE			SCOTLAND	
Year	Total number of farms	Number owner-occupied	Percentage owner-occupied	Acreage owner-occupied	% of total agricultural acreage	% farms owner-occupied	% agricultural acreage owner occupied
1940	9859	3091	31.4	210,534	24.3	23.6	31.3
1950	9594	3563	37.1	233,130	38.0	27.1	39.8
1960	7957	4489	56.4	355,226	57.8	38.2	51.2
1970	5458	3666	61.7	592,912*	62.1*	46.4	56.8*

* includes rough grazings, rather than just crops and grass

a more limited growth in owner-occupied farms. In Aberdeenshire, this continued to be mainly in the east of the county, where nearly all the parishes in the districts of Turriff and Deer showed a noticeable increase in owner-occupied farms between 1945-70. The change was less in Ellon district where several main estates still survived. On Donside, the changes were more variable from parish to parish, with the extent of owner-occupiers more limited in mid-Donside and non-existent in upper Donside. On Deeside, owner-occupation also made very little progress. Most significant was the sale by the Aberdeen Real Estate Company, which had acquired the former Finzean lands in Lumphanan during the 1930s, of the farms to the tenants in the 1950s. Otherwise, the other main development was after 1970 when the 9,000 acre estate of Drum in Lower Deeside was broken up. This had been owned by the Irvines since the 14th century and in 1975, following the death of the last of the line, the farms were sold to the tenants, while the castle and policies went to the National Trust for Scotland.

The agricultural statistics for 1940-1970 suggest a resurgence in the increase of owner-occupied farms during the 1950s and 1960s. However, unlike the statistics between the wars, these figures give no clear indication of the number of tenants buying their own holdings. Instead, against the background of a sharp decline in the total number of farms, the statistics reflect the post war policy of estate owners to take their farms 'in-hand' under their own direct management. This practise, and the lack of any details on the extent to which it has occurred, means that agricultural statistics do not accurately reflect the gradual, but significant increase in genuine owner-occupiers.

The number of landowners in Aberdeenshire with 100 acres or more rose from 339 to 1,046 between 1872 and 1970. This suggests an

Fig 6.5   The Structure of Landownership in Aberdeenshire,
1872 and 1970

Size Class	Number of Estates		Percentage of County	
(Acres)	1872	1970	1872	1970
Over 100,000	1	—	11.1	—
50,000-100,000	4	4	24.1	21.3
20,000-50,000	5	3	9.6	6.3
10,000-20,000	14	5	14.8	5.0
5,000-10,000	25	17	14.3	9.2
1,000-5,000	106	110	19.6	22.8
Totals	155	139	93.5	64.6

increase of at least 600, even allowing for the fact that the 1970 figure incorporates some duplication through ownership in more than one parish. This steep increase in numbers, like the sharp decline between 1667 and 1771, occurred almost exclusively amongst small landowners. The number of landowners with 1,000 acres or more stayed remarkably constant between 1872 and 1970 (Fig 6.5).

The relative constancy in the number of these estates in Aberdeenshire between 1872-1970 was not matched by the total acreage held between them. The proportion of Aberdeenshire owned by estates of 1,000 acres or more declined from 93.4% in 1872 to 64.6% in 1970. This fall of nearly 30% was, as, with the number of owners, a net figure. The 1,000-5,000 acre estate bracket, which had marginally increased in number by 1970, also slightly increased their percentage of the county. Thus, estates larger than 5,000 acres were the significant break-point. Their total acreage fell by 32% from 73.8% to 41.8% between 1872-1970.

These changes in Aberdeenshire closely matched the changes in Scotland as a whole. The average proportion of Scotland's counties held by owners with 1,000 acres or more fell from 92.8% in 1872 to 62.8% in 1970 (Fig 6.6). The extent of the decline did vary from county to county, but this had little effect on the overall pattern of landownership within Scotland. The counties with the highest percentage held in estates of 1,000 acres or more in 1970 still tended to be the counties that had had the most concentrated patterns of landownership in 1872 (Fig 6.7). This distribution of estates in the 19th century had itself reflected a longstanding pattern from the early centuries of feudal landownership in Scotland.

Fig 6.6   Landownership in Scotland 1970:
Owners with 1,000 acres or more by County with comparison of
percentage held in 1872 (excluding the Northern Isles)

COUNTY	Area of County (acres)	Number of owners ≥ 1,000	Acreage held by these owners	1970 % of county	1872 % of county
Aberdeen	1,261,333	139	814,821	64.6	93.4
Angus	559,090	80	397,400	71.1	87.9
Argyll	1,990,522	184	1,242,100	64.4	98.7
Ayr	724,234	43	189,100	26.1	85.6
Banff	403,054	39	227,000	56.3	98.0
Berwick	292,535	46	160,300	54.8	84.0
Bute	139,711	12	100,200	71.1	98.5
Caithness	438,943	34	350,200	79.8	99.5
Clackmannan	34,860	13	26,800	76.9	82.0
Dumbarton	154,462	30	103,300	66.9	78.5
Dumfries	688,112	52	437,300	63.6	88.0
East Lothian	171,044	30	75,800	44.3	86.9
Fife	322,856	41	111,300	34.5	63.7
Inverness	2,695,094	141	1,748,300	64.9	99.5
Kirkcudbright	574,024	22	90,300	15.7	87.6
Kincardine	244,248	47	178,100	72.9	89.9
Kinross	52,392	9	18,400	35.1	26.7
Lanark	574,473	34	172,700	30.1	74.0
Midlothian	234,389	34	115,700	49.4	74.5
Moray	304,931	30	203,900	66.9	96.5
Nairn	104,252	11	76,800	73.7	96.6
Peebles	222,240	27	112,800	50.8	95.8
Perth	1,595,804	248	1,396,100	87.5	93.6
Renfrew	143,829	20	59,100	41.1	74.7
Ross & Cromarty	1,997,254	102	1,654,600	82.8	80.2
Roxburgh	424,564	47	248,700	58.6	90.1
Selkirk	171,209	25	97,900	57.2	92.3
Stirling	288,345	60	143,700	49.8	73.6
Sutherland	1,297,803	53	1,139,500	87.8	99.7
West Lothian	76,855	17	37,900	49.3	61.9
Wigton	311,984	46	268,200	86.0	96.0
Totals	19,068,807	1723	11,918,521	Average 62.8	Average 92.8

*Fig 6.7   Percentage of land owned by owners with 1000 acres or more
Scottish Counties 1872 and 1970 (excluding Northern Isles)*

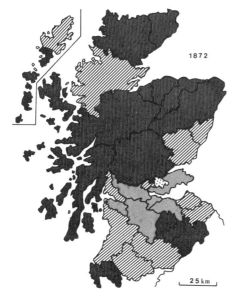

KEY

OVER 90 %

75 – 90 %

50 – 75 %

25 – 50 %

0 – 25 %

Landownership in Scotland

The decline of 30% between 1872 and 1970 in the extent of land held by owners of 1,000 acres or more, represented a reduction in their combined holdings of 366,000 acres in Aberdeenshire and over 5.5 million acres amongst all the Scottish counties. The ownership of these acres went in two main directions. They were either broken up amongst owners with less than 1,000 acres or else they passed into some form of public or state ownership. The relative importance of these two directions varied from county to county, but were shared approximately 50:50 for Scotland as a whole. In Aberdeenshire, the growth of small owners was more important and accounted for around 75% of the change. This represented an increase of over 250,000 acres in the extent held by owners with less than 1,000 acres and was due nearly entirely to the growth of owner-occupier farms, with the majority (150,000 acres) going to them during the twenty years 1920-1940.

The spread of urban development accounted for approximately 1.5% of Scotland's land area between 1872 and 1970, still leaving over 97% of Scotland's total land area classified as rural. This 1.5% was equivalent to 5% of the area lost by the larger landowners. The average annual loss of agricultural land to housing, roads and urban spread during the 5 years before 1970 was nearly 6,000 acres. These losses, however, tended to be very localised and had little effect on the wider pattern of landownership. The losses were mainly in the urban fringe, where the scale of landownership had usually already declined.

While proximity to urban centres had tended to reduce the scale of landownership, it had often strengthened the position of surviving estates through the sale of rural houses and cottages. This sale of surplus buildings has become a widespread practise amongst estates, as it raises ready capital without any noticeable impact on the estate's overall acreage. This trend has had correspondingly little influence on the wider pattern of landownership over Scotland's 19 million acres, but nothing has done more during the last 100 years to introduce new property owners into rural areas.

The growth of public or state ownership between 1872 and 1970 was very significant in Scotland, which has a higher percentage of its land area in this form of ownership than either England or Wales. In 1872, central and local government and various public agencies owned approximately 37,164 acres in Scotland or 0.2% of the land area. Most prominent were the Commissioners of Supply, the Commissioners of Northern Lighthouses, the War Department and the Board of Trade while, at a local level, the main cities like Edinburgh, Glasgow and

Fig 6.8   Public Landownership in Scotland, 1970s*

Category	Approximate Area (acres)
Local Authorities (New Towns)	178,000
Nationalised Industries	126,500
Crown Estate Commission	85,500
Forestry Commission	1,473,000
Department of Agriculture & Fisheries Scotland	429,500
Ministry of Defence	47,500
Other Government Departments & Agencies	64,000
Total	2,404,000

* (For a map of state owned land in Scotland at 1970 see H.E. Bracey, *People and the Countryside* RKP 1970.)

Aberdeen were significant landowners. By 1970, public ownership involved around 2.5 million acres or 13% of the land area, the majority of this being held by the Forestry Commission (F.C.) and the Department of Agriculture and Fisheries for Scotland (D.A.F.S.) (Fig 6.8). The list is not exhaustive and excludes some bodies that are not directly state related like the National Trust for Scotland with around 80,000 acres, held inalienably in trust through legislation.

The distribution of the publicly owned land in Scotland had been influenced by historical and political variables, as much as any factors of land quality. The greatest extent of public ownership has always been in the Highlands, involving about 15% of the land there in 1970. In Aberdeenshire, the 1970 figure was approximately 90,000 acres or 7% of the county, close to half the national average. This principally reflected the greater opportunities or requirements for D.A.F.S. and the F.C. to acquire land elsewhere in Scotland.

The extensive acreage held by D.A.F.S. mainly resulted from the settlement schemes that operated in Scotland between 1897-1955. These involved the acquisition of private estates to make crofts and other tenanted small holdings more available. The relative abundance of small landholdings in Aberdeenshire earlier this century meant the county was not a priority area for the D.A.F.S. schemes. The programme therefore had little impact in Aberdeenshire, with only a few small areas being taken over for subdivision, for example, Fortie (811 acres) in 1919, Balmedie (300 acres) in 1933 and Auquhorthies (290 acres) in 1938. One of the main factors that limited the F.C.'s expansion in the uplands of Aberdeenshire was that the estates in

Fig 6.9   Forestry Commission Lands in Aberdeenshire 1970

ENTIRELY IN ABERDEENSHIRE		PARTIALLY IN ABERDEENSHIRE	
Name of Forest	**Acres**	**Name of Forest**	**Acres**
Alltcailleach	4,461	Bin (with Banff)	8,730
Bennachie	7,656	Deer (with Banff)	6,734
Clashindarroch	16,406	Durris (with Kincardine)	6,655
Kirkhill	2,965	Midmar (with Kincardine)	7,109
Pitfichie	7,562	TOTAL	29,228
Tornasheen	10,030		
TOTAL	49,080		

these areas owned some of the richest sporting moors in Scotland. An indication of the F.C.'s lands in Aberdeenshire is given in Fig 6.9. Over half of this acreage was acquired in the first 15 years of the F.C.'s existence up to the mid-1930s.

The public agency for nature conservation sites, the Nature Conservancy Council, has acquired surprisingly little land in Aberdeenshire. Deeside in particular, has a number of extensive sites of national and international importance. However, the N.C.C. settled for lease agreements with the large estates that own these sites. The National Trust for Scotland's involvement in Aberdeenshire has also been restricted, being mainly focused on the county's distinctive castles, in comparison with the tracts of landscape the N.T.S. manage in some parts of Scotland.

The growth of public or state ownership in Scotland since the 1870s accounted for about half of the acreage lost from the total held by estates larger than 1,000 acres by 1970. However, while the extent of Scotland held by these estates dropped from 92.8% to 62.81, the increase in state owned land meant that these estates' share of privately owned land in Scotland remained much higher. In 1970, three-quarters of all privately owned land in Scotland was still held in estates of 1,000 acres or more, half in estates of 5,000 acres or more and a third in estates of 20,000 acres or more.

These statistics indicate that the pattern of estates has been less disrupted than the decline in their extent might suggest. Fig 6.10 shows the numbers of largest landowners holding the different percentage levels of the total areas of Scotland and Aberdeenshire in 1872 and 1970. The dilution of this pattern during that 100 year period was relatively limited, even without restricting the comparisons to privately

Fig 6.10 Percentage of land held by largest landowners in Aberdeenshire and Scotland 1872 and 1970

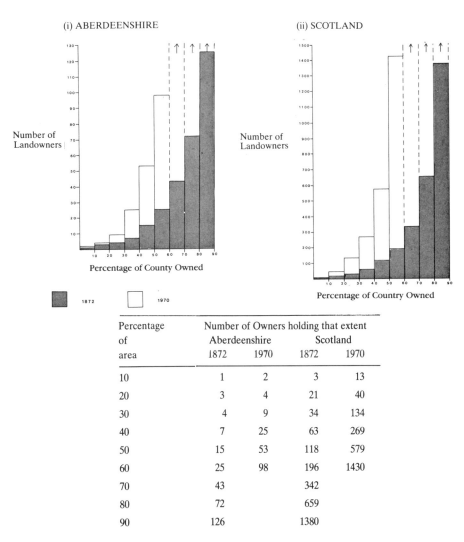

Percentage of area	Number of Owners holding that extent			
	Aberdeenshire		Scotland	
	1872	1970	1872	1970
10	1	2	3	13
20	3	4	21	40
30	4	9	34	134
40	7	25	63	269
50	15	53	118	579
60	25	98	196	1430
70	43		342	
80	72		659	
90	126		1380	

owned land. This dilution, the reduction of acres of landownership into smaller units, had made most progress at the bottom end of the scale. However, it had not penetrated far up the traditional hierarchy of progressively larger estates. For example, the increase between 1872-1970 from the 15 to the 53 largest estates sharing 50% of Aberdeenshire, was the same order of proportional increase as the rise from 339 to around 1,000 owners with 100 acres or more. However, it still left a very concentrated pattern of landownership. In 1970, as in 1872, 50% of Aberdeenshire was owned by less than 0.05% of the county's population.

This concentrated pattern of landownership in Aberdeenshire in 1970 closely matched the position in Scotland as a whole. Similarly, the composition of the owners of Aberdeenshire's larger estates also reflected the wider Scottish position. There had been some notable changes in the owners and acreages of Aberdeenshire's largest estates since 1872 (Fig 6.11), but the owners in the 1970s still included representatives from most of the main periods in the 900 year history of feudal landownership. This continuity is illustrated by the fact that a quarter of the estates in Fig 6.11 were still held by the same families that had owned these lands for 400 years or more.

Two of the families in the list had received their lands in Aberdeenshire from Bruce in the 14th century. The Farquharsons of Invercauld were an old Scottish family that had been displaced from their Speyside lands by the Comyns, Bruce's enemies. The Gordons, ancestors of the Earls of Aberdeen and the present owners of Haddo, were an Anglo-Norman family that first became established as landowners in Scotland in the Borders in the 13th century. Invercauld estate was still the same size in 1970 as 1872, but Haddo had declined to one tenth of its 1872 extent.

Two other estates in the list date from the 15th century. Lord Forbes' ancestors had owned land in Aberdeenshire since at least the 12th century, longer than any Farquharsons or Gordons. However, the lands of Castle Forbes were not obtained by the first Lord Forbes until 1423. These lands are the focus of the present estate, which by the 1970s was half the acreage it had been in 1872. Abergeldie estate was acquired by the second son of the 1st Earl of Aberdeen in 1485. The present laird is the 21st Gordon of Abergeldie. The estate was leased to the Royal Family for much of the period since 1872, with the Royal Family also buying the 6,000 acres White Mounth area from Abergeldie in 1955.

The Farquharsons of Finzean, number 16 in the list, originally stem from the Farquharsons of Invercauld, though they claim to be now the senior line of Farquharsons. They acquired their first lands in Birse parish in 1580 and added Finzean itself in 1609. They expanded their lands throughout the 17th and 18th centuries, with the estate at its greatest extent in the first half of the 19th century. The estate is now

Fig 6.11   The 25 largest estates and their owners, Aberdeenshire 1979

Estate	Owner	Acreage
1. Invercauld	Capt A.A.C. Farquharson	87,500*
2. Dunecht (with others)	Viscount Cowdray & the	
	Hon C.A. Pearson	65,600
3. Mar Lodge	Harlow and Jones (Investment) Ltd	65,000*
4. Balmoral, Birkhall	H.M. Queen & Trustees of	
& Delnadamph	Balmoral Estates	50,370*
5. Glen Tanar	Hon Mrs Jean Bruce	29,150*
6. Mar	Capt A.A.A.D.M. Ramsay	25,143*
7. Dinnet & Aboyne	J.M.M. Humphries (with Trusts)	25,000*
8. Candacraig	Falconer Wallace	15,000
9. Tillypronie	Lord Astor of Hever	13,500*
10. Glenmuick	Sir Ian Okeover-Walker Bt.	13,000*
11. Bogney	Alex G. Morison	11,700*
12. Abergeldie	John Gordon	10,200
13. Douneside	MacRobert Trust	9,000*
14. Littlewood	D. Maclean & Littlewood Trust	8,460*
15. Towie Barclay	Aberdeen Endowment Trust	
(with others)	(Trustees of)	8,008*
16. Finzean	Alison Farquharson & family (with Trusts)	7,900*
17. Slains	Sir Richard Sutton	7,574*
18. Fyvie	Sir A.G. Forbes-Leith Bt. (with Trusts)	7,720*
19. Glenkindie	Fairview Estates	7,300*
20. Haddo	Trustees of Haddo	7,047*
21. Glenbuchat (North)	W. Tulloch	7,000
22. Ballogie & Balnacraig	Col J. Nicol & family	6,000*
23. Allargue	Lady Forbes	5,940
24. Castle Forbes	Lord Forbes & family (with Trusts)	5,660*
25. Towie (part)	Mr & Mrs Smith	5,500*

Total acreage: (40% of Aberdeenshire)   504,072

(*=confirmed by owner)

half the size it was in 1872. The Morisons of Bogney have also held their estate since the 16th century. Their greatest expansion was in the mid 17th century, when marriage to the widow of Viscount Frendraught brought those lands into the Morison family. Bogney, at 11,700 acres, showed an increase of 1,500 acres between 1872-1979.

Only one of the 25 largest estates has been with the family of the present owner since the 17th century and only one from the 18th century. In both cases, the present owners are also married to members of other traditional landowning families that have lost most of their Aberdeenshire lands. Allargue estate, number 23 in the list, became the property of a separate branch of the Farquharsons in the first half of the 17th century. The present owner, Lady Forbes, is a Farquharson of Allargue who married Sir John Forbes of Newe, the ancient Forbes estate lower down Donside from Allargue which had all been sold except for a house and a couple of acres by 1927. Mar estate, the focus of the lands of the pre-feudal Mormaers of Mar, was first sold in 1739, as a result of the Earl of Mar's leading role in the Jacobite Rising of 1715. The estate was bought by the Earl of Fife, a member of the same original family from which the Farquharsons were also an off-shoot. The present owner of Mar is the successor through marriage of the Earls of Fife. The estate has been dramatically reduced over the last century and the owner now lives at the other end of Aberdeenshire in Cairnbulg Castle, with his wife Lady Saltoun, another representative of an old but much reduced landowning family.

The lands of another six of the 25 largest estates in Aberdeenshire in the 1970s were acquired by their families in the 19th century. The most famous of these are the Royal estates of Balmoral and Birkhall bought by Queen Victoria in 1852. This century the Royal Family have added Delnadamph (7,600 acres) in the mid-1970s, as well as the 6,000 acres from Abergeldie in 1955. 1852 was also the year the Nicols acquired the estates of Ballogie and Balnacraig. In 1862, they added the estate of Midstrath and the only change since was the addition of Auchabrack farm in the 1930s from Finzean estate. In 1883, Littlewood estate, formerly a Forbes possession, was bought by the MacLeans while, in 1889, Fyvie estate, an old Gordon property, was acquired by the Forbes-Leiths. Fyvie, which had been held by Gordons for 200 years after it was forfeited by the Earl of Dunfermline in the 1690s, has been reduced in size by nearly half this century. The 1880s were also when the MacRoberts started to build up their Douneside estate, which is now managed by a Trust following the death of three sons at the time of the Second World War. The Aberdeen Endowments Trust, part of the financial background to Robert Gordon's College in

Aberdeen, first acquired their Aberdeenshire lands in the late 19th century.

The 11 other estates in the top 25 were acquired or built up by their present owners during this century. Most of these estates derive from the break-up of large 19th century estates, such as those of the Earl of Fife, Marquis of Huntly and Forbes of Newe. The most prominent of these new owners in Aberdeenshire have been the Cowdrays. After their purchase of Dunecht in 1905, they added a wide scatter of estates to give them a total holding of more than 64,000 acres or over 100 square miles of Aberdeenshire. Most of their land is in the south and west of the county and much of it has now been handed over from Viscount Cowdray to his younger son, the Hon Charles Pearson. Not included in their acreage is Castle Fraser estate (3,600 acres), which was bought by Lord Cowdray in 1921. This is owned by Mrs Smiley, a member of the Cowdray family, who also owned part of Glenbuchat until recently. The Glenbuchat estate had been part of the Earl of Fife's lands and was acquired in 1901 by the Barclay-Milnes. Part of the parish is still owned by Mrs Sole, a daughter of that family, but three other portions were sold for death-duties and are now owned by the F.C., Viscount Cowdray and W. Tulloch.

The estates of Aboyne and Dinnet and Glen Tanar result from the break up of the Marquis of Huntly's estate. The Barclay-Harveys acquired the former in 1901 and the present owner, a nephew of the last laird, is a descendant of that family. Glen Tanar was bought in 1905 by Mr Coates of the thread firm. He was created Lord Glen Tanar and the present owner is his granddaughter. Candacraig was established out of Newe in 1900 and is still held by the Wallace family, who first acquired it, though some parts are now being sold off. The widely separate estates of Glenmuick and Slains have a connection because the Walkers, who had bought Glenmuick from the McKenzies, bought Slains from the Gordons of Cluny in 1942. The Walkers, a traditional English landowning family, sold Slains in 1964, but still retain Glenmuick.

Glenkindie estate was long the property of the Leiths who, since the 17th century, had been the Leiths of Freefield, Towie and Kildrummy. Glenkindie itself was sold on the death of the last Leith line in the 1970s to the English based company, Fairview Estates. The other parts of the original estate had been split off much earlier and contribute to two other estates in the top 25. These two estates, numbers 9 and 25 in the 1979 list, had both been acquired since 1945. Tillypronie estate had been built up by Lord Royden between the wars and was bought from

Fig 6.12 Sketch map of main estates in Deeside District, Aberdeenshire (1979)

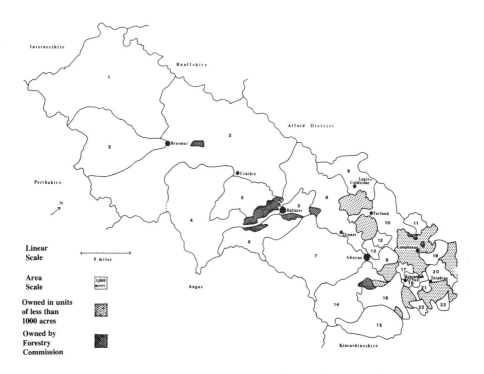

Numbers 1-23: estates of 1000 acres or more, which between them own c.364,000 acres or 95% of the 382,127 acres in the nine parishes of Deeside District:–

Estate	Owner	Estate	Owner
1. Mar Lodge	Harlow and Jones Ltd	12. Coull	Alastair Lilburn
2. Mar	Capt A.A.A.D.M. Ramsay	13. Aboyne and Gellan	Earl of Aboyne
3. Invercauld & Monaltrie	Capt A.A.C. Farquharson	14. Birse	Hon Charles Pearson
4. Balmoral & Birkhall	H.M. the Queen	15. Finzean	Alison Farquharson & family
5. Abergeldie	John Gordon	16. Ballogie & Balnacraig	Col John Nicol & family
6. Glenmuick	Sir Ian Ikeover-Walker	17. Dess	William Calvert
7. Glen Tanar	Hon Mrs Jean Bruce	18. Findrack	Andrew Salvesen
8. Dinnet, Kinnord & Dessmuir	J.M.M. Humphrey & Trusts	19. Kincardine O'Neil	Brigadier B. Bradford
		20. Learney	Thomas Innes
9. Tillypronie	Lord Astor	21. Mid Beltie	Trustees of James Allan
10. Douneside & Cromar	MacRobert Trust	22. Sluie	R. Strang-Steel
11. Corse	Trustees Lt Col Forbes	23. Campfield	Dickinson Trust (Cowdray)

*Fig 6.13   Further estates held by traditional landowning families
amongst the fifty largest landowners in Aberdeenshire 1979*

Estate	Owner	Acreage
Monymusk	Trs Sir Francis Grant Bt. with Trusts	5,486*
Udny & Dudwick	Udny & Dudwick Estates	5,000
Cluny	Cluny Estates	5,000
Auchmacoy & Auchleuchries	Capt D. Buchan	4,935*
Barra & Straloch	Major F. Irvine & family	4,250*
Knockspock	Knockspock Estate Co.	2,995*
Hatton	D.R.M. James-Duff & family trusts	2,700*
Brucklay (with others)	J.A. Dingwall-Fordyce	2,340*
Esslemont	Capt Woolridge Gordon	2,319*

(* = confirmed by owner)

his executors by Gavin Astor in 1951. A few weeks later Gavin Astor added Towie estate, which he bought from the Lumsdens of Clova. In 1971, Gavin Astor succeeded his father as Baron Astor of Hever. Hever, their main estate in England, has subsequently been sold. The final estate in the list is Mar Lodge. This major new estate was sold out of Mar Estate in the late 1960s to Harlow & Jones Investments. This company is controlled by the Panchaud brothers who are Swiss but claim a Scottish connection.

Thirteen of the largest estates in Aberdeenshire in the 1970s were in Deeside (Fig 6.12). Balmoral and Invercauld estates also extended into the neighbouring counties of Angus and Perth, while the Dunecht estate lands in Deeside were only a part of their Aberdeenshire lands. More of the Dunecht lands were in Donside and, between them, Aberdeenshire's two major valley systems provided the locations for 19 out of the 25 largest estates in the county in 1979. However, both the distribution of large estates and traditional landowning families extend beyond the uplands of west Aberdeenshire and the ranks of the 25 largest landowners.

As with the top 25 estates in 1979, a third of the largest 50 estates were held by families who had owned the same lands for 200 years or more (Fig 6.13). Similar examples of old landowning families are found down through the ranks of all Aberdeenshire's estates of 1,000 acres or more. The distribution of 100 of these estates shows their spread across most of the county (Fig 6.14).

Fig 6.14   Distribution of one hundred of the largest
landholdings in Aberdeenshire owning over 60%
of the county between them, 1979

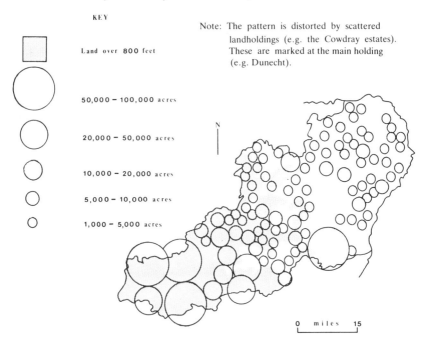

KEY

Note: The pattern is distorted by scattered
landholdings (e.g. the Cowdray estates).
These are marked at the main holding
(e.g. Dunecht).

Land over 800 feet

50,000 – 100,000 acres

20,000 – 50,000 acres

10,000 – 20,000 acres

5,000 – 10,000 acres

1,000 – 5,000 acres

0   miles   15

This distribution within Aberdeenshire reflects the longstanding progression, where changes in the pattern of landownership have advanced from the lowlands in the east to the uplands in the west of the county. Between the 1870s and 1970s, the most significant changes were mainly in the east. Changes in Deeside only resulted in bringing the proportion of the district held by estates of 1,000 acres or more down to around 94%, the average for the whole county in the 1870s. This survival of larger estates in the areas of lowest land values itself reflected the wider changes in Scotland up to the 1970s. Nowhere more so than in the Highlands and Islands covering nearly half the area of Scotland. There, just 35 families each with estates of 36,000 acres or more, still held one third of all the privately owned land.

Since 1970, there has been little change in the pattern of landownership either in Aberdeenshire or Scotland as a whole. The general trends of the previous 100 years and more have continued, with a gradual reduction in the sizes of the largest estates and continued slow increase in the number of smaller owners. During the 1970s, there were some conspicuous elements in the land market. The purchase of estates by overseas buyers attracted particular attention. One survey of 66 of these purchasers, involving over 0.25 million acres, showed that 30 of the buyers were Dutch, 12 were Americans, 12 were from Arab countries and 12 from other countries. It was estimated by the government-appointed Northfield Committee in 1978 that foreign nationals had acquired about 2% or 320,000 acres of Scotland's agricultural land. However, foreigners acquired significantly more land than this in Scotland. Scotland's agricultural land excludes 3 million acres of the total land area and over 75% of all foreign purchases in the 1970s were of sporting estates in the Highlands, where there is a limited extent of agricultural land.

In the Lowlands, another feature of the land market in the 1970s was the purchase of agricultural land by financial institutions. These bodies acquired, according to the Northfield Committee estimates in 1978, about 1.2% of all agricultural land in Britain, or over 0.5 million acres. However, this was mainly in England. In Scotland, the North-east was a favoured area. The British Rail Pension Fund was, for example, a prominent purchaser in East Aberdeenshire during the 1970s, while other bodies such as the Pension Fund Property Unit Trust acquired around 2,000 acres in the same area.

A third prominent purchaser of estate land during the 1970s and particularly during the first half of the 1980s, has been the commercial forestry companies, notably Fountain Forestry, the Economic Forestry Group, Tilhill and Scottish Woodland Owners Association. These companies typically do not acquire the land to own it themselves, but for clients wishing to invest in a forestry. As a result, single purchases of land may be divided between a number of different owners, either private or institutional, the institutional buyers preferring to purchase established plantations rather than bare ground for planting. The investment character of these purchases means that the private owners, as well as the institutions, are absentee owners. One survey for Sutherland showed that 70% of these purchasers had addresses in London or the Home Counties, and in many instances the purchasers have never seen the land they own in Scotland.

Overseas purchasers, financial institutions and forestry investors have all attracted attention as prominent elements in the land market. However, as with conspicuous groups in previous centuries, their penetration of the pattern of landownership has been relatively limited. The forestry purchasers, for example, acquired less than 2%

of the land area of Scotland between 1975 and 1985. In many instances, it is also the case that one wave of new purchasers acquire a significant percentage of their land from the previous group. This conforms to the historical tendency for land that has changed hands once in the recent past to be more likely to be sold sooner than land that has been held for a longer period. Estates in absentee ownership are also more likely to come onto the market than those with a resident owner. The present wave of forestry purchasers have exaggerated these tendencies, because the various tax advantages at the different stages of the forestry cycle encourage changes in the ownership of the land involved.

Behind the prominence of the transient phases of new owners, the traditional pattern survives with little change since 1970. The relative constancy of this pattern, dominated by a small number of large estates, has survived for centuries, let alone the most recent decades. Since the 1970s the changes were less than during most of the previous decades back to the 1870s. The political and economic position of landownership has continued to improve since the 1950s and there is little reason at present to anticipate any significant changes to Scotland's concentrated pattern of landownership.

Chapter 7

Commonties

Millions of acres of common land survived the first five centuries of feudal landownership in Scotland. However, by the end of the 19th century, nearly all this common land had been added to the private estates of Scotland's landowners. In Lowland Scotland and the fringes of the Highlands, the overwhelming majority of these areas of common land were commonties. These commonties were uninhabited areas that ranged in size from a few acres to several thousands of acres. The Scots Parliament passed a series of Acts during the 17th century that allowed commonties to be divided out between neighbouring landowners and this led to a rapid reduction in the extent of commonties during the 18th and 19th centuries. The division of Scotland's commonties was the third major addition to the estates of private landowners following the acquisition of the Crown's and then the Church's lands during the previous centuries. The history of these commonties represents a major episode in the development of Scotland's pattern of feudal landownership.

Commonties originated as areas of land over which traditions of common use predated the arrival of feudalism. However, the 17th century legislation for their division, although part of the Scots law of common property, defined them as a form of private property. Under these Acts commonties were not classified as genuine commons as these are normally understood. Commonties were not "no-one's land" or public property and, in legal terms, differed from the "pro indiviso" or indivisible rights in genuine common property. The rights to use a commonty were held to go with the neighbouring lands. The rights in a commonty were therefore held to belong to the neighbouring landowners and the right to a share of a commonty at its division could only be derived from the title to these individually held lands. This made commonties into appendages of such private property and meant that, by definition, commonties were simply the undivided private property of neighbouring, though not necessarily adjacent, landowners.

This definition of commonties was an essential pre-requisite to enable them to be legitimately shared out between landowners from the 17th century onwards. The definition's validity dated from the arrival of feudalism in Scotland. The laws of feudalism started from the premise that all land had to have a land-lord and, by presuming and promoting rights of property over the whole countryside, the original establishment of feudalism converted all common land in Scotland into a form of private property.

During the early feudal period, the Crown's specific demesne was very extensive and the grants of land to the Church and other main landowners often conveyed huge tracts of countryside. The areas that were subsequently designated as commonties occurred within these massive territories, as well as in the general demesne. They were areas with ancient and strong traditions of communal use that were irrevocably built into the annual cycle and subsistence economy of the rural communities. The existence of these areas was acknowledged in charters by the convention which evolved of conveying wide and unspecific rights as a matter of course in land grants. Prominent amongst these would be phrases like "with all commons, commonties, common woods and common grazings". No areas might be named or identified in any way and, indeed, none might exist near the lands conveyed.

This legal style developed as a matter of precaution and practise to ensure that a landowner's tenants still had access to the resources they depended upon and which might be outside the new landowner's personal estate, in an area of traditional communal use. The fact that these phrases later became interpreted as conveying definite rights over specific areas to the landowners, was one of the main reasons why the division of commonties during the 18th and 19th centuries gave rise to such a wealth of legal disputes.

Commonties were therefore not simply remote relics that had survived outside the earlier feudal grants. The firmly rooted communal use of these areas continued unimpeded within the initial wide grants of land and then, as the number of landowners increased before the 17th century, they survived as areas of shared property. It was the increase in the number of landowners that led to these areas becoming conspicuous as areas of common property, not just common use. They had been submerged into feudalism as areas of shared use and emerged as areas of shared property. It was the traditional common use by local populations that maintained these areas and which became converted into the landlord's right to claim a share in them as private property.

The distribution of commonties resulted from patterns of landownership being superimposed on patterns of communal use. It was not possible for tenant populations to be cut off from these vital areas, so that areas which had been used by a single owner's tenants continued to be used by these tenants after they had become the tenants of several landowners.

A crucial distinction could emerge when one owner possessed the superiority of any of the other owners' lands. In these cases, the vassals rights in the common land were just rights of servitude (use), not rights of property. If one owner possessed the superiority of all the lands which had rights in an area of common use, then the area was not a commonty. Similarly, the dramatic contractions in the number of landowners during the 17th, 18th and 19th centuries meant that many commonties disappeared without recourse to the process of division. This was because all the rights of property in each of these commonties had become possessed by a single proprietor. The commonty thus became individually held private land. While some commonties were shared between only two landowners, many commonties, particularly the larger ones, became associated with whole parishes and were shared by all the landowners in these parishes.

Parishes owed their origins to the same general period as the arrival of feudalism. The comprehensive coverage of parishes absorbed all local communities and the common land used by local inhabitants often became associated with the parishes' organisation. Parishes were administered by the local landowners, or the heritors of the parish. The people who used the uninhabited commonties were all tenants of these heritors, or else of the heritors of any other parish that shared the commonty. The heritors' authority over these people and the parish as a whole, meant that the heritors administered the commonties. These commonties were seen originally as parish land, but with the consolidation of feudalism and the institution of private property, the commonties became described as the heritors' land. The ambiguity of this transfer was still reflected in many comments in the Statistical Accounts of Scotland in the 1790s and 1840s. As late as this, many reporters still described surviving commonties as "belonging to the parish", while the law had long since conveyed these lands to the landowners in the parish.

The first Act of the Scots Parliament to provide a legal framework for the division of commonties was in 1608. However, this Act was intended to protect commonties against encroachment and it only allowed the common possession to be broken if all the parties agreed. The division of commonties had already taken place prior to this Act as, for example, at Lennoxlove in 1500 and at Echt in 1560. The 1608 Act and the subsequent commonty legislation were attempts to regulate what was already happening.

There was a second Act in 1647, which dealt specifically with commonties in the Lothians, Lanarkshire and Ayrshire. This Act enabled commonties to be divided where there was only agreement between a majority of the heritors involved and the consent of the superiors. Finally, in 1695, there was the third and main Act for the division of commonties. All subsequent divisions were under this Act and it was this Act which was responsible for the disappearance of Scotland's commonties during the 18th and 19th centuries.

The 1695 Act allowed a commonty to be divided at the instigation of a single pursuer or "any having an interest", whether the other parties agreed or not. The Act laid down the procedures to be followed to give an equitable division of the commonty and provided the basis of the process of commonty divisions. The only relevant pieces of legislation to follow the 1695 Act were in 1852 and 1877. In 1852, an Act of Sederunt was established by Scotland's Court of Session to tidy up the procedures of the 1695 Act. An 1877 Act, reiterated in an Act of 1907, transferred the business of division from the Court of Session in Edinburgh to local Sheriff Courts, if the land involved was of less than £50 annual rent or £1,000 value. The divisions continued, however to be governed by the 1695 Act, which still remains in force at the present time.

The process of division established by the 1695 Act was straightforward. It was instigated by a pursuer submitting their claim to a share in the commonty at the Court of Session and producing title deeds to substantiate this. All other parties were then called upon to defend their rights with all necessary proof. The various claims were assessed by a judge, who then appointed a local commissioner to arrange the division if all the legal aspects were in order. The commissioner hired surveyors to measure and map the commonty and then the commissioner divided the commonty between the heritors with regard to both the quantity and quality of the land. The shares were calculated in proportion to the valued rents of the properties through which the heritors derived their rights and were allocated on the basis of proximity to these other holdings. The division was then recorded and registered in the Court of Session, the costs of the operation being shared in proportion to the lands received. The whole procedure, from the raising of the action to the final settlement, might only take a couple of months, when no legal disputes needed to be contested.

Disputes could arise out of the allocation of the shares from the division. For example, the traditional shared use or souming of the commonty was organised on the basis of an equal share for all, yet the division was calculated on the basis of the extent of land owned outside the commonty. This frequently resulted in gross inequalities in the final shares, with the smaller landowners always being the victims. Similarly, parts of the commonty might prove indivisible and an agreement would have to be reached over their fate. For example, a valuable stone quarry was usually left undivided and leased to an external party, the income then being divided between the heritors. The allocation of shares was, however, not the most common problem. The great majority of disputes arose from the initial issue of who had rights to a share in the commonty. Many commonties produced long and expensive law cases, which required all the parties involved to dig down to the bottom of the family deed chest for ancient grants. The precise terms of these titles and what rights they conveyed, needed detailed legal decisions which were frequently contested. Many commonties were in and out of the courts for a century or more. The simple procedures of the 1695 Act were in marked contrast to the maze of legal complexities and ambiguities that emerged through its application.

Most of the legal disputes stemmed from the fact that even the legal authorities had to conclude 'It is not at all times easy to ascertain whether the right be a right of common property, or merely a right of servitude'. A servitude provided a right of use, but neither a right to a share in the division nor the right to sue for a division. The distinction between the rights of property and servitude was frequently not apparent in the history of a commonty, as the possessors of the different rights would still have shared the area equally. The distinction only became relevant at the time of a division and derived from the wording of the title deeds of each claimant. Even with the most genuine claim to a right of property, the wording and terms of the title deed were often very ambiguous. This reflected the limited nature and origins of the claim of any proprietor to a share in the commonty. The old deeds seldom named the commonty in question and the whole issue depended on subtle interpretations of the stylistic conventions used in the heritors' titles to their own privately held lands. The distinction could hinge on, for example, whether the title to their own land said 'with parts, pendicles and pertinences', or 'with parts, pertinences and privileges'. The former conveyed a right of property in an adjacent commonty, while the latter would be interpreted as a right of servitude.

The fact that estates might have changed hands several times led to complications in the titles and the need to scour the earlier titles for some phrase that might establish a claim as a right of property. An additional complication was that superiors, who might have long ago feud out all their lands relating to a certain commonty, could still claim through their superiorities a right to a share in any division. Thus, those who had been making no use of the commonty could receive a share, while other traditional users might receive nothing from a division, if their title was deemed merely one of servitude. However, rights of servitude did continue to exist over the divided out shares of the former commonty. There was no legal process for removing these rights and no way the holders could be compelled to dispose of them. However, it was usual practise for these rights to be exchanged outside the courts for an area of land in outright ownership. The normal formula for this arrangement was the number of stock previously grazed, irrelevant of the extent of area used, and was a strong incentive to put as many stock as possible on the commonty. This exchange of servitudes for an agreeable amount of land could result in new divisions over each of the divided portions of a former commonty, so that it became fragmented beyond recognition.

The one interested party who did not require to be called or cited by law, were the tenants or actual users of the ground. Sometimes they were taken along as witnesses to give evidence on the past uses of a commonty. However, more usually, the only indication the tenants had of an impending division was a pre-ambulation or walking of the boundaries by the landowners or their agents, followed by the arrival of the surveyors. Surveyors soon became recognised as agents of misfortune and records survive of them being driven off by local 'mobs' with sticks and stones. The tenants had little or no prospect of any benefit from a division and they stood to lose their means of survival when the division was carried through and the land put beyond their reach. The tenants who were called as witnesses, were usually the oldest local inhabitants and have themselves left, in their statements, some of the richest accounts of the central role commonties had in the rural economy.

A heritor's rights in a commonty allowed all possible resources to be exploited, unless forbidden by law or reserved to the Crown, and the tenants had the privilege to use any of these resources through their heritor, excepting any reserved by the heritor for personal use. The scope of these all embracing rights means it is not possible to make any exhaustive list of all that a commonty could provide or all the uses they have been put to in the past. However, the list of assets that local communities obtained from commonties is in marked contrast to the impression conveyed by heritors when commonties were being divided. Then, commonties were described as just barren wastes, peripheral to the needs of agriculture. Yet the collective fermtouns of Scotland's subsistence agriculture, which survived in northern areas into the nineteenth century, were a traditional arrangement that could not survive without the resources provided by a commonty. A commonty could provide many of the resources needed by a community at no cost apart from the inhabitants' own labour. The commonty also offered a degree of flexibility to meet fluctuations in population or food supply, that was not possible within the formal restrictions of privately held land. The image of commonties as barren wastes was the perspective of the landowning class, who were seeking to do away with commonties and the fermtoun structure they served.

A commonty usually offered the complete set of building materials: stone and the clay for mortar, timber for roofing and fixtures, the fail and divot for walls and roofs, a range of thatches, whether heather, broom, rushes or bracken, and in some areas, slate. The commonty met all fuel needs: usually peat and turf, with gorse and broom, sometimes wood and, in central Scotland, occasionally coal. The commonty was fully incorporated into the agricultural cycle: for nearly half the year, between May and October, it was the site of the sheilings and grazings; it offered a reserve of arable land where an extra crop could be taken and it supplied a range of fertilisers, of which turf was the most typical but which might include limestone, marl or kelp. The fishing and hunting on a commonty might be reserved by the proprietors, but these areas traditionally offered opportunities in those lines for the local population, even when forbidden by the landlord. The commonty also offered the range of blossoms, berries and sap crops available from the native vegetation and which had many traditional uses as foods, drinks and medications. Commonties offered areas of free access whether for comings and goings, markets and fairs, or other events, particularly those needing to be more out of sight from the authorities, such as sectarian preaching. Commonties could be used for bleachfields or offer scope for mill dams to supplement summer water supplies downstream. The list of resources could be extended, as could the variety of uses for the types of resources already mentioned. It is easy to forget the full range of uses that were made of natural resources that are of little direct material value today (e.g. heather, bracken) by communities which were then living off such limited resources.

This extensive use of commonties contradicted the landowners' assertion that these areas were barren wastes. However, the landowners also claimed that these commons suffered from over-exploitation and cited the ancient dictum that 'that which is common to the greatest number has the least care bestowed upon it' (Aristotle). Yet this argument, the traditional 'tragedy of the commons', had a limited bearing on the circumstances of commonties. Commonties were not a 'free for all' like genuine commons. Their use was covered by sets of rules that were, unlike the legal subtleties of servitude or property, well established and understood locally. Aspects of these regulations may have grown out of traditions as old as the commonties themselves and some are still suggested by modern practises over the common grazings of crofting townships. The system of rules for commonties included a conventional souming or sharing of the principal resource uses between the heritors and this was repeated amongst the tenants on each estate. For example, with grazing, the heritor's extent might be shared between the tenants in proportion to the valued rents of their holdings, a specific stock total decided for each, with recognised equivalents for different species (for example, five sheep equalling one horse or cow). Other rules were even more clear cut. No one, whether tenant or heritor could make financial profit out of the commonty. The resources of the commonty were solely for personal uses and individuals could not, for instance, cut timber for sale or rent out grazing to someone else. Such rules were also backed up by the recognised procedure whereby any heritor seeing another infringing the commonty had the right and responsibility to sue them at law.

The use of the over-exploitation argument was deceptive as it disguised the reasons for the introduction of the commonty legislation. As the modern authority on commonties, Dr Ian Adams, observed in his doctoral thesis: 'On the whole, these Acts were passed to strengthen the concept of private property rather than simply providing agricultural improvement'. These Acts were part of a wider body of 17th century legislation aimed at rationalising and clarifying the hold of landowners on their land. The momentum that existed for this was reflected in the re-concentration in the pattern of landownership that started during that century.

The gradual progression in the commonty legislation during the 17th century, from requiring consensus to allowing the instigation of the division by a single pursuer, does reflect a certain inertia or caution but there can be no suggestion of these changes being foisted on the landowners. In the 17th century, landowners had virtually complete control of both the Scots Parliament and the legal profession. The progression reflected a growing confidence and a gathering momentum in the new values of landownership.

This initial reason for the commonty legislation is sometimes camouflaged by later events. The origins of the Acts were different from the causes behind the rapid increase in the division of commonties from the mid 18th century onwards. The motivation was no longer the idea or fashion of removing the sometimes legally ambiguous commons as part of consolidating an estate. The motivation had become economic and, as a result, by the mid 18th century, the opinion of the landowning classes had become unanimous in condemning commonties as wasteful relics of the past that impeded modern progress.

The profitable development of commonties was not possible unless they were divided. The rules governing the use of commonties expressly forbade earning personal profit from their resources and were also a strong disincentive to improving any part of a commonty for one's own use. Any such expenditure could be exploited by the tenants of other landowners and, if a division should subsequently occur, no compensation was allowed for improvements in the calculation of the shares to be allocated. It was only after a share had been secured as unimpeded private property that the agricultural, forestry and sporting use of these areas could be profitably developed. In the second half of the 18th century, all these landuses were offering increasingly strong financial returns.

These economic incentives were resulting in Improvement on individually held lands and led to a sharp increase in the number of commonty divisions from the 1760s. For the next 100 years, the prospect of profit provided the momentum for commonty divisions. Less and less favourable land became involved and, by the 1870s, the huge bulk of Scotland's commonties had been divided. Fig 7.1 plots the known records of submissions for divisions against their geographic location. The resulting overall south to north diffusion is similar to the pattern recorded for the spread of Improvement in general. However, as with the spread of Improvement, the progress of the divisions was not a simple result of diffusion. At the local level, a complex range of factors were involved.

Fig 7.1   Diffusion of Commonty Divisions Northwards 1695-1900
(each dot represents one summons)

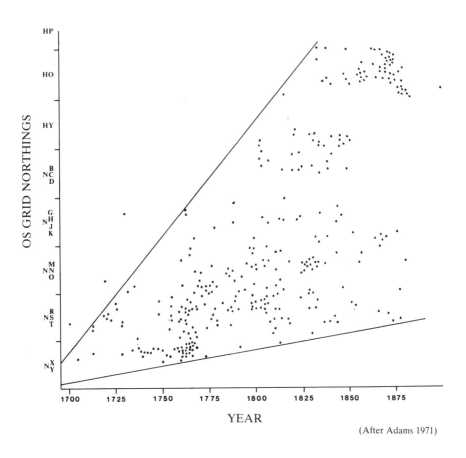

(After Adams 1971)

Two important factors emerge from the individual records of commonty divisions. Firstly, that the most frequent cause of a commonty to be brought to a division was encroachment. Secondly, that the instigators of the divisions were normally the smaller landowners and those who had made least progress with Improvement on their own individually held lands.

These conclusions do not point to the fact that the smaller landowners were responsible for the encroachment. As Rankine suggests in his 'Laws of Landownership in Scotland': "All history shows that the tendency has been the very opposite — for the powerful to encroach on the ancient rights of the weak". The records support this, as the pursuers were invariably the injured parties and recourse to the law was the only effective defence to rescue their rightful share of a commonty before it was illegally enclosed by more powerful neighbours. The legal processes also show that encroachment had often already substantially reduced the acreage that came up for division. It was a similar pattern of encroachment that forced the 1828 Act allowing the division of Crown Commons.

The division of commonties in Aberdeenshire tended to occur later than further south in Scotland, although they followed the same pattern. Within the county, the divisions of commonties around Aberdeen and in the more arable eastern half of the county generally occurred earlier than in the more upland west. The upland commonties were normally larger, so that in Donside major commonties were coming up for division in the final period before the 1870s. (See Appendix C).

By contrast with Donside, the western parishes of Deeside, Aberdeenshire's other main upland valley system, have no records of any divisions. The two parishes of Upper Deeside cover 260,000 acres (105,206 ha) and have always been Highland parishes, culturally as well as physically. Their lack of any divisions is a feature shared with most Highland parishes.

Fig 7.2 shows the distribution of the main areas in which former commonties have so far been recorded. Their absence from most of the Highlands is very conspicuous and this poses one of the main unresolved questions in the history of Scotland's common lands. Why are there so very few records of common property from the Highlands, particularly when this is the region in which the inhabitants' ancient traditions of common rights of use have lasted longest?

In the case of Upper Deeside, many of the old charters contain references to commonties. These usually appear to be the unspecified commonties of legal convention, but some are specifically named. One conspicuous reason for the limited number of commonties is the area's history of largescale landownership. The quarter of a million acres in Upper Deeside had originally all been part of the lands of the Earls of Mar and, by the 17th century, the number of landowners had reached a maximum of 40. Most of these were small landowners and by the 19th century, the number of landowners was back down to just five.

Within this concentrated pattern of landownership, very few areas of common land became shared by landowners. The limited extent that did emerge tended to involve rights of servitude, not property, because

Fig 7.2 Distribution of Commonty Records

 The main areas in which commonties have been recorded

(After Adams 1971)

of the common superior of most of the landowners. Finally, the major reduction in the number of landowners between 1695 and the 1850s resulted in the disappearance of areas of common property. Some areas also seem to have been removed by trade-offs between the major landowners to avoid the expense of formal divisions through the Court of Session in Edinburgh.

This explanation for Upper Deeside is not sufficient by itself to explain the wide lack of records of common property in the Highlands. The history of feudal landownership in the Highlands is quite distinctive from that in the Lowlands. The Highlands missed out on many of the early phases of feudalism and feudal titles to land only became widespread in the Highlands at a later date, which will also have influenced the position of common lands. It is very likely that the late penetration of feudalism into the Highlands, combined with the Gaelic culture it encountered, resulted in many distinctive aspects to the history of common lands there. The development of feudalism in the Highlands, however, remains poorly researched at present.

Another question associated with the history of commonties is the impact of their division on the local populations that had made use of them. The problem is that these divisions were only one element in the major changes affecting rural communities in Lowland Scotland at that time. The seriousness of the impact was also affected by the timing of the division relative to these other changes. The later divisions tended to have a less severe impact, as the local population was likely to have already been depleted by changes in farm structure, landuse practises and settlement patterns. In each locality, the impact also depended on the extent and character of the commonty involved.

However, these factors only affected the degree of the impact. The evidence shows that the divisions of commonties had a profound effect on rural communities during the 18th and 19th centuries. Subsistence agriculture could not survive without access to the resources that the commonties traditionally supplied. Some local populations still had the common use of adequate resources on their landlords' individually held lands. However, in other areas, the evidence suggests that the loss of commonties was a major factor in forcing local inhabitants to abandon the way of life that had sustained the generations before them and join the mass of people leaving the Scottish countryside.

Chapter 8

Other Types of Scottish Commons

Commonties are only one of the seven main types of common land recognised in Scotland. All the other types are similar to commonties, in that their origins predate the arrival of feudalism. Three of them, common mosses, runrig and scattalds, are forms of undivided common property identical or similar to that of commonties. Another two of the types, crown commons and greens and loans, are more akin to genuine commons. The final type, burgh commons, is a collective designation for common lands that could incorporate one or more of the other types.

(i) Common Mosses

A moss is a wet area where peats could be dug and many were used in common by local inhabitants. Common mosses were the same form of shared property as commonties and could be divided under the same legislation. Most commonties included a moss and the 1695 Act, recognising the difficulties of dividing a moss equitably, allowed for mosses to be left out of commonty divisions. This meant that many common mosses only became independent commons as the result of a division. If a moss was divided, the method of calculating the shares for the various proprietors could vary. After the quantity and quality had been assessed, the shares of the respective heritors might be decided by the lengths of their other lands facing on to the moss or else by giving lengths of linear cutting face in proportion to the valued rent of their other lands.

The problems of dividing mosses and their exclusion from so many commonty divisions, suggests that a relatively large number of common mosses may still survive. The common status of these mosses has often

116

gone un-noticed, because they have been of little use since the decline of peat cutting in Eastern Scotland. Recently, however, their afforestation potential and their botanical interest have focussed new attention on them. Both the Forestry Commission and Nature Conservancy Council have encountered common mosses when trying to acquire land during the last few years.

(ii) **Runrig**

Rigs were narrow strips of cultivated land, sometimes up to 40 feet wide. The rigs were ploughed in from each side to build them up and to emphasise the furrows in between them, which provided for drainage. Traditionally, adjacent rigs would be used by different cultivators and the rigs were periodically re-allocated between them. This system was known as runrig, from the Gaelic Roinn-nuth or 'division run'.

Lands lying runrig were invariably associated with an area of rough ground or hill land that was also shared in common. These two elements were central to the traditional system of farming in Scotland before the Improvements of the 18th and 19th centuries. In many areas, the redistribution of the rigs died out before the use of the rigs themselves, but both survived longest in the Western Highlands. Latterly, the land involved was owned by a single proprietor and it was only common use, not common property, that was involved.

Originally, many areas of runrig, together with their shared hill ground, were held by two or more proprietors. Each owned a number of rigs which were interspersed with the rigs of the other owners and each owner had an undivided share in the ownership of the common hill. The common hill was thus a commonty and the runrig lands equivalent to a commonty on arable land.

The Scottish Parliament passed an Act for the division of runrig lands in 1695, the same year as the Act for the division of commonties. The Act enabled landowners to apportion the rigs between themselves into consolidated holdings. The rigs were allocated in proportion to the value of the heritors' other lands and divided so that the share of each was closest to their other lands. These principles were the same as were established for the division of commonties, but the process was easier as the division could be heard by a Sheriff or Justice of the Peace. This also made the process more susceptible to local influence by the more powerful landowners.

The division of runrig lands between landowners had occurred extensively before the 1695 Act, which simply formalised the arrangements involved. As arable land, runrig land was more valuable than hill ground and the division of runrig lands had always tended to precede the division of commonties. Placing the division of runrig lands within the jurisdiction of local courts reflected this position. It was not until the 19th century that the division of commonties was transferred to the local courts.

(iii) Scattalds

Scattalds are a type of common land found in the Shetland Isles and are associated with udal, as opposed to feudal, tenure. Under udal tenure, land can be held by possession without any written title deed and is free of all the burdens and conditions associated with feudalism.

Udal tenure in the Northern Isles is a legacy of Norse influence and, though some land there has been feudalised, udal tenure still survives as an exception to feudal landownership in Scotland.

Scattalds are areas of common lands shared between different owners and, because of their similarity in that respect to commonties, can be divided under the 1695 Act for the Division of Commonties.

It appears that historically there were at least 127 scattalds in the Shetland Isles (for details see Knox 1980). Fifteen or more of these still survive, making them one of the most conspicuous examples of common land in Scotland today.

(iv) Crown Commons

These commons were held directly by the Crown and are thought to have originated out of the once extensive Royal Hunting Forests. The rights to use these commons were less restrictive than with commonties. They were most heavily used by the populations of the localities in which they occurred, but anyone unconnected with the area could also use them.

Crown commons did not come within the commonty legislation, so that the owners of neighbouring lands had no rights to instigate a division. However, a growing problem of encroachment on Crown commons forced an Act in 1828 to allow their division and the land was normally shared out between the adjoining landowners. There appear to be no Crown commons left in Scotland. Some did survive into this century, when their administration was taken over by the Crown Commissioners.

One of the last Crown Commons was 'The Shooting Greens' which straddled the boundary between the parishes of Birse (Aberdeenshire) and Strachan (Kincardineshire). It was never formally divided and some legal ambiguity still seems to exist. Various rights over the Shooting Greens were granted by the Crown Commissioners to the Forestry Commission, when the Commission bought one of the neighbouring estates in the 1930s. However, the common was still extensively used by a wide range of people and, up until the 1950s, one of Deeside's last flockmasters spent much of the winter there between September and May, with his flock of 400-500 ewes. It was only in 1960, after two other adjoining estates were persuaded to give up their rights in the common, that the Forestry Commission planted their first trees on the Shooting Greens.

(v) Greens and Loans

A green is a small area of common land usually closely associated with a settlement, whether a town, a village or single clachan. These greens provided an area where cows could be milked, markets and other events held, garments bleached and a host of other common and communal activities carried out.

The extent of shared ownership in greens is not known and no records exist of any divisions. However, most appear to have been genuine commons to the extent that only the Crown held any title to them. Some of these greens still survive, but the fate of most is unknown. Many appear to have been simply absorbed into an adjoining estate, when their common use declined. 'The Green' in Aberdeen's city centre is one of the best known examples in North-east Scotland.

One specific type of green were the stances associated with traditional routes and drove roads. These were situated for overnight stops and at river crossings. Several examples of these greens still survive in Aberdeenshire. The green opposite the Potarch Inn, at the Inchbare crossing of the Dee, is still a common, although now managed by the local authority. Anyone waiting to be ferried across the Dee was entitled to the use of this ground and, after the bridge was completed in 1814, the area continued to be used as a market and feeing stance. A similar site exists four miles further south along the Cairn o'Mount route and is situated across the Feugh from the Feughside Inn.

The term loan is more normally associated with a route, rather than any particular area along the way. A loan was a common route through private property to and from an area of common or some other 'public' place. The distinction between this and a right of way was that the loan was itself common land and not just a privilege of use. The fate of most loans is unknown, although some have survived as rights of way. The former existence of some is indicated by the placenames like Loanhead and Loanend that occur frequently in Aberdeenshire and the rest of Scotland. Most loans fell into disuse with the disappearance of commonties, the end of the drove trade and the lapse of peat cutting, and appear to have been absorbed into the adjoining estates.

(vi) **Burgh Commons**

Burghs were established in Scotland from the 12th century onwards by both the Crown and local barons. Most burghs, but particularly the Royal Burghs established by Crown charters, received extensive territories and wide privileges for the use and support of their inhabitants.

These property rights and privileges of use held by the burgh or its feuars were the burgh commons. They did not represent a single type of common land, but might encompass the full range of Scottish commons: commonties, common mosses, runrig lands and common hill land, greens and loans. These areas and other rights, like fishing privileges, were not always held exclusively by the burgh, but might also be shared in common with the owners of land outside the burgh's boundaries.

Few burgh commons survive in Scotland today. However, a clear indication of their former great extent can be found in the Reports of the House of Commons Select Committee on the Royal Burghs of Scotland for 1793, 1819, 1820 and 1821, and in the 1832 Report of the Commissioners into the State of Municipal Corporations in Scotland. These investigations were prompted by the growing concern and scandal at the disappearance of burgh commons and resulted in the Burgh Reform Act 1833. The reports showed how the loss of the burgh commons stemmed in large part from an Act of the Scottish Parliament in 1469. This suppressed the popular election of Councils and lead to the dominance of the burghs by local landowners and wealthy merchants. The evidence in the reports shows how these landowners and merchants, with their relations and allies, had appropriated the burgh commons to themselves through generous grants and cheap feus. By the early 19th century, they had stripped the Scottish burghs of virtually every acre of common land and all the associated rights. The records for the burghs of Aberdeenshire are not as comprehensive as for many other areas, but examples of the disposal of their landed assets do illustrate the pattern throughout Scotland.

The Royal Burgh of Kintore had disposed of all its lands to the family of Keith (Lords of Kintore) and held 'now no property' in 1833.

In the adjacent Royal Burgh of Inverurie, the Magistrates alienated burgh property to the value of £2,449 between 1794-1833. In 1833 the Council still collected feu duties of £73.6.8 and in 1836 there was still a Burgh muir consisting of about 35 acres of heathland. This muir was situated on the north side of the turnpike to Huntly.

By 1833, Keith had nothing left and Huntly had lost its charter that gave privileges of common pasturage, fuel and quarries. These rights had by then been withheld by the Duke of Gordon for 'about sixty years' and so had become lost. Both Peterhead and Fraserburgh had lands invested in their feuars and these seem to have survived better. Peterhead had originally obtained the Moss of Peterhead, fisherlands, certain commons and pasture rights from the Earl of Marschial in 1593 but the commons were divided in 1772. Fraserburgh still possessed its burgh links in 1836 and they were used for pasturing cattle, a herring curing station, for rope works, timber yards and similar accommodations for ships' stores. In 1681, the feuars of Rosehearty had common pasturage in certain lands, a share in the Commonty of Cairnhill and in certain mosses, including 'the large moss called the Red Moss'. All these rights had been lost by 1811, except the privilege of casting fuel and divot from the Red Moss.

In 1819 it was reported that Aberdeen 'once possessed land which extended many miles in circuit round Aberdeen, granted by the Kings of Scotland, for the use of the Town'. The most famous of these grants was Bruce's 1319 charter which gave Aberdeen its 'Freedom Lands'. In 1459, Aberdeen owned, amongst other lands, those of Rubislaw, Countesswells, Hazelhead, Forester Hill and Northfield Cruieffs. These extended altogether to about fourteen miles in circumference and the Town also possessed the valuable salmon fishings on the Dee and the Don. However, in 1551, the then Magistrates procured a new charter from the Crown to allow them to dispose of the common property by perpetual feus. This resulted in the immediate loss of the fishings and much of the land for insignificant amounts to a favoured few. Most of the remainder went over the following centuries with, for example, £19,444 of heritable property being disposed of between 1793-1817.

The Aberdeen story incorporates references to several specific commons around the town. Taylor's 1773 plan shows a small common moor (under 10 acres) north of Bonnymuir House, which is now part of the Royal Infirmary grounds (Ordnance Survey reference NJ 9206), and a loan to the south that terminated at Loanhead farm. An 1820 plan shows the Commonty of Whitemyres (142 acres) and notes add that about 400 acres to 'the north side of the Skene' (NJ 9006) had been feud from the Commonty in 1756 to different purchasers, together with 'Summerhill' (of unknown extent). Thus this town moor extended to more than 542 acres in 1756. Another eighteenth century plan shows the Commonty of Old Aberdeen situated south of Dubford farm (NJ 9412), and stretching east towards the coast. This Commonty appears to have originally incorporated Corse Hill and Perwinnes Moss (NJ 9312), both of which are identified as the Commonty of Perwinnes (229 acres) in an 1867 summons for division. The action was unsuccessful and in the 1890s two local books were written about the Commonty. They trace its history from the Bishopric of Aberdeen to the incorporation of the old ecclesiastical burgh into the modern City of Aberdeen. The Commonty suffered encroachment by agricultural reclamation in both World Wars and by the 1970s, its ownership had passed to the occupier of Perwinnes farm.

Chapter 9

Common Land in Scotland Today

Modern authorities are consistently of the opinion that very little, if any, common land still exists in Scotland. This suggests that common land in Scotland is a closed chapter and a subject that can be left to the history books. However, this 'theory of extinction' appears to be based on confusion and perhaps should not be accepted with the same degree of confidence with which it is usually asserted.

The confusion has been between genuine or 'pro indiviso' commons and common land as a form of private property. Whether genuine commons as such have ever existed in Scotland, is a mute question. Throughout the last nine centuries of feudal landownership, all common land in Scotland has either belonged to the Crown or has been an accessory to privately held lands. The freedom of access to the Crown's commons has made them appear closest to genuine commons. However, even any small and remote green unassociated with any private property, has always been eligible for management as part of the Crown's estates.

There has always been a popular tradition that has tried to contradict this legal reality. In the past, this has been reflected by the calls of land agitators and other radicals for the landowners to produce their title deeds, in the belief that these titles would show no claim to areas of common land as these belonged to the people as a whole. A striking instance of this was the popular opposition to the division of the common lands of Bennachie, the prominent and symbolic hill that dominates the lowlands of Aberdeenshire. A long sequence of direct actions against the division culminated in the famous raid on Bennachie, organised by the Aberdeen Trades Council in 1889. Their opposition collapsed defeated, when the bitter truth of Bennachie's legal status as undivided private property was eventually realised.

Landownership in Scotland

The distinction between genuine commons and common property was not a problem for more informed observers in the 18th and 19th centuries. For example, in 1794, when tens of thousands of acres of commonties still existed in Aberdeenshire, James Anderson reported in his 'General View of the Agriculture of Aberdeenshire', that 'Of commons, in the strict sense of the word, I know of none in the county. Indeed, they are scarcely known in any part of Scotland.'

However, during the 20th century, a confusion has arisen over the position of common land in Scotland. This has resulted from a tendency to link the extensive past records of the divisions of common land with authoritative historical quotes about the lack of common land. This has suggested that no common land survives in Scotland when, in fact, the quotes were only referring to 'pro-indiviso' commons.

The history of common land in Scotland has always been concerned with common property rather than genuine commons and recognising the confusion that has developed over the nature of common land in Scotland undermines the view that it has all been lost. The issue becomes one of establishing to what extent common land does still survive in Scotland. The lack of any systematic record or register of landownership in Scotland means this question can not be easily answered. However, as the survival of some scattalds, common mosses, burgh commons and greens indicates, areas of common land clearly do exist.

The records researched by historians are unlikely to reveal much directly about surviving common land. More historical research, particularly in local sources such as Sheriff Court records, will certainly locate more former common lands and improve knowledge of their operation. However, these historical sources only tend to supply negative information, as they are usually based on records of the divisions of common lands. The exceptions are those instances involving unresolved disputes. There is a surprisingly high number of these, typically involving commonties, amongst the records available to date.

Many of these cases were still unsettled, and therefore the land undivided, by the 1860s and 1870s. As there has been no division of a commonty in the Scottish courts for 100 years, it is very hard to believe there was time for all these cases to be returned to the courts and successfully settled. It is equally unlikely that all Scotland's commonties were completely divided down to the last few acres. A conclusion reinforced by their former great extent and the small extent of known divisions in some localities.

The records of commonty divisions, particularly in upland districts, do not suggest these were the last scraps being tidied away. The abrupt end of recorded divisions in the late 1870s appears much more plausibly explained by the economic and political changes that occurred then, than by any theory that there were suddenly no commonties left.

The economic downturn that started in the 1870s swiftly reduced the financial incentives for spending money in the Courts on a division, particularly if there was any risk of a prolonged and expensive case, for example, over an area that had already been disputed. These economic constraints against further commonty divisions were also reinforced by the political climate that developed at this time. Rural unrest in Scotland during the 1880s was threatening the landowners' control of their individually held lands and few landowners are likely to have been looking to provoke the situation with commonty divisions.

The 1876 Commons Act in England had already limited the scope for further divisions of the commons down south. In Scotland, William Alexander concluded in 1889 that the shift in political opinion was sufficient to ensure that it would no longer prove possible for a commonty to be divided successfully. William Alexander was a particular authority on rural life in North-east Scotland and it is in areas like the North-east where commonties are most likely to have survived. Divisions came later in the north and were latest in the upland districts, so that not all will have been undertaken before the process came to an abrupt end during the late 19th century.

Several surviving commonties appear to have been uncovered in recent years. For example, as reported by Dr Roger Millman in his survey of Scotland's estate boundaries and by Forestry Commission Acquisition Officers. However, to confirm these areas as commonties would require a detailed examination of the title deeds of the respective parties, in order to distinguish genuine commonties from areas subject to extensive servitudes.

The Forest of Birse Commonty in Aberdeenshire (see Appendix C, part ii) is a good example of the complexity that may be uncovered by such investigations. The rights of property in sport are shared by two landowners, while all the other rights in the Forest are shared as rights of servitude between the many Heritors of the parish of Birse. The rights in the Forest have been frequently contested in the past, although there have been no court cases for 150 years. Confusion and disagreements still exist between the parties involved over the operation of the Forest but, so far, the potential expense of any legal clarification has been sufficient to maintain a measure of co-existence. The Forest of Birse Commonty involves over 9,000 acres (3,644 ha.) and illustrates how commonties can still be operating over extensive areas in the Scottish countryside.

The complex arrangements governing the Forest of Birse do not strictly conform to those in a commonty and, although the sporting rights were informally divided in the 19th century in an out of court settlement, the Forest of Birse itself can not be divided under the 1695 Act for the division of commonties.

The 1695 Act requires that, for any land to be classed as a commonty, the rights in that land have to conform to a set of legal criteria. Commonties are not simply areas of land on the map, but a distinctive legal arrangement or form of feudal tenure. The present state of understanding within the legal profession on this form of tenure, seems no better than the current ignorance of the extent of commonties in the Scottish countryside.

Lawyers are familiar with commonties as a word in most estate title deeds, as it still remains in these as a constant element of conveyancing convention. However, the lack of legal cases involving commonties during the last 100 years, means few lawyers have any experience of them beyond the short accounts of commonties in 19th century legal dictionaries. In the only related case this century in 1929, when the land in question was decided not to constitute a commonty, the Lord Justice Clerk concluded, 'It is difficult to find, in the institutional writers or in the earlier cases, a clear and comprehensive definition of a commonty. Probably its features were familiar then, though they are archaic now.'

This lack of a positive definition for the tenure of commonties reflects their origin within the feudal system. They have only ever been defined by default, principally through the provisions of the 1695 Act for their division. However, the legal arrangement represented by commonties is not an isolated or anomalous component in Scotland's system of landownership. All property ownership is shared to some extent under this feudal system and the common property of commonties has its place amidst the spectrum of legitimate arrangements or tenures within Scotland's complex feudal landownership.

The shared character of all property is inherent in the hierarchical structure of feudalism. Within this structure, the basic pattern is for the Paramount Superior and a vassal, or the Paramount Superior, one or more subject superiors and a vassal, to all have proprietorial interests in any piece of land. Superiorities or the 'dominium directum' can be held by one or more superiors, one above the other. By contrast, the fee or 'dominium utile' can only be held at one level, that of the vassal in actual possession of the land. At that level, it is quite normal for the 'dominium utile' to be shared equally or unequally by more than one individual or owner.

Commonties represent a situation where the 'dominium utile' of an area is shared equally in an undivided state between more than one owner and held directly, with no other superiors below the Paramount Superior. The essential tenurial characteristic of the commonties is that the owners only derive the right to a proprietorial share in the land by virtue of their title to other lands within the general locality.

In this way, commonties are just one feudal permutation amongst many. Perhaps the closest parallel to commonties is provided by the status of freshwater lochs. These cover around 2% of Scotland and are still considered as the undivided private property of the surrounding landowners. If a loch falls wholly within the lands of a single proprietor, then they have sole possession. However, where the land around a loch is owned by more than one proprietor, they share the loch. In theory, the property of each owner extends into the loch from the frontage of their own lands up to some mid-point, where it meets the property of the other common owners. In practise, this is normally impossible to determine and the rights are therefore shared in common so that, for example, any owner has the right to fish or boat over the whole surface.

Freshwater lochs provide an example of how other elements in the Scottish landscape, apart from commonties, required special arrangements to bring them within the overall feudal system. In many ways, the main difference between freshwater lochs and commonties is simply that a method was never discovered for dividing lochs into separate shares.

The 1695 Act for dividing commonties remains on the statute books to the present day. It is one of very few Acts of the Auld Scots Parliament not to have been repealed during one of the periodic Statute Law Revisions to remove redundant old Scots legislation. This Act can not be repealed because commonties still survive, most conspicuously as scattalds in the Shetland Isles. It is perhaps doubtful whether this feudal law should ever have been applied to scattalds because of their udal basis. The freedom this Act has given for nearly 300 years to a single pursuer to force the division of a commonty, might also be considered due for revision.

To replace the 1695 Act would require some perspective on the present extent of commonties and also necessitate drawing up a modern legal definition of commonties and the principles governing their operation. This is unlikely to occur except as a part of a wider reform of feudal tenure in Scotland. In the meantime, a test case involving a commonty may result from the spread of afforestation in upland Scotland. The history of common lands in Scotland is not over, although it remains to be seen what the future holds for the few surviving commonties, scattalds, common mosses, greens and loans.

Chapter 10

The Patterns of the Past

This book has given an outline of the historical development of the pattern of feudal landownership in Scotland, to illustrate the relationship between the present pattern and the patterns of the past.

Any examination of this relationship is constrained by many factors, not least the lack of information available on both the modern and historical patterns of landownership. In particular there is no official record of the contemporary pattern. The only clear indication this century of the number of landowners in Scotland and the sizes of their properties, has come from the work of Roger Millman and John McEwen.

Roger Millman carried out a survey of estate boundaries in Scotland in 1970. John McEwen then used this to calculate the number of estates of 1,000 acres or more in each Scottish county and to provide lists of the names of the landowners and estates involving 5,000 acres or more. The maps of Roger Millman's survey are deposited in the Scottish Record Office in Edinburgh and John McEwen's book "Who Owns Scotland" was published in 1977, with a second edition in 1981.

Perhaps not surprisingly, John McEwen's book contained many inaccuracies in its lists of estate owners' names and the acreages of particular estates. However, beyond these individual details, the overall accuracy of the results has been confirmed by local studies, including the one for Aberdeenshire undertaken for this book. All the available evidence also suggests that there has been very little overall change since Millman and McEwen's 1970 dateline and that their work remains a fair representation of the present estate structure and its distribution within Scotland.

The present pattern of landownership in Scotland is only the most recent moment in the evolution of the pattern of feudal landownership in Scotland during the last nine centuries. Comparing the present pattern with the patterns at different periods in that long history indicates a relatively high degree of continuity in the numbers and sizes of estates, as well as their distribution within Scotland and the composition of their owners.

One of the most conspicuous features of this continuity has been the small number of large estates that have always dominated the pattern. Fewer than 1,500 private estates have owned the majority of Scotland's land throughout the last nine centuries. It has been around this core that the overall numbers of landowners have fluctuated.

The dominant trends have been the increase in the number of owners before the 17th century, followed by the decline until the 19th century and the increase in the number of landowners since that time. This has been the main fluctuation in the history of feudal landownership in Scotland. An impression of these changes is given in Fig 10.1 for Aberdeenshire, which has followed the overall Scottish trends closely. The availability of additional details and more strictly comparable information would produce a more irregular line. However, this would not alter the basic form represented. For example, with the speculative line plotted for the first five centuries, more knowledge of different rates of increases and minor fluctuations would only add detail to the overall increase in owners between the 12th and 17th centuries. Similarly, for the period since the 17th century, there would be more minor fluctuations like those associated with the Jacobite Risings of 1715 and 1745 while, for example, 1900-35 would stand out as a period of greater increase compared with 1935-1970.

The start of the line in Fig 10.1 at around the 12th century can be viewed as a low point in the number of landowners, resulting from the concentration in the control of the land that occurred with the establishment of feudalism. It is also possible, at the other end of the line, that the number of landowners might start to decline again from its present high point. For example, the financial institutions that have already been active in the Scottish land market, have the purchasing power to acquire all the land coming up for sale in Scotland. There may never be the incentive for them to do this and political pressure might restrict the extent to which they were allowed to do this. However, they do illustrate how a new re-concentration could occur.

The 1,500 largest estates in Scotland have retained their longstanding hold on the majority of the land, despite the increases in the numbers of landowners since the mid 19th century. The distribution of those

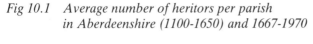

*Fig 10.1   Average number of heritors per parish
in Aberdeenshire (1100-1650) and 1667-1970*

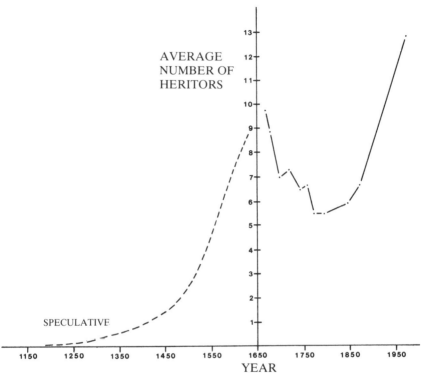

estates within Scotland is also still concentrated in those areas that have traditionally been most dominated by large estates: the Borders, the North-east and the Highlands. Similarly, the counties in central and west central Scotland, where large estates have the least hold, have had a relative abundance of landowners for centuries. The present pattern of landownership in Scotland still matches closely the earlier patterns stretching back through the last nine centuries and, in some instances, the differences between counties can be traced back into pre-feudal times.

The continuity in the regional variations in the pattern of land-ownership in Scotland, means that individual counties may have occupied a similar position in the wider Scottish pattern for many centuries. While the overall Scottish statistics have incorporated these variations, so the statistics for the individual counties can reflect

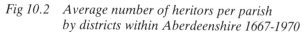

*Fig 10.2   Average number of heritors per parish
by districts within Aberdeenshire 1667-1970*

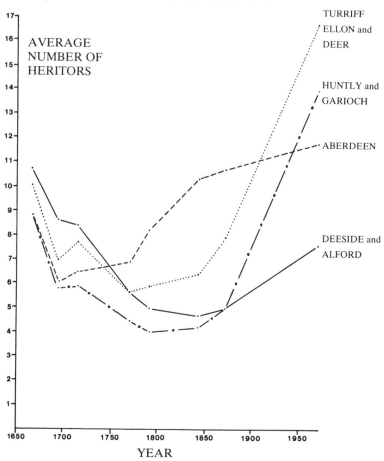

longstanding variations between the different districts within these counties. This is illustrated in part for Aberdeenshire in Fig 10.2. This subdivides the line in Fig 10.1 to give an impression of how the changes in the numbers of owners operated differently in the various districts of the county.

In Fig 10.2 it can be seen that the district around Aberdeen was the first to show an increase in the number of landowners, due to its proximity to the town. In modern times, the spread of urban development around Aberdeen has limited the scope for increases in the number of rural landowners. In comparison, Deeside and Alford districts did not show any net increase in their number of landowners for 150 years after this trend had emerged near Aberdeen. These districts have also yet to show an increase in landowners equivalent to that which has occurred on the land in the districts of East Aberdeenshire.

These variations between districts themselves incorporate the different patterns of landownership in the parishes that make up each district. Each local area has had its own pattern of landownership throughout the feudal era, incorporating its own distinctive elements of continuity and change. Fig 10.3 provides an example of a representation of this for a single parish. In this Aberdeenshire parish of Birse, there has been little growth of owner-occupied farms or state ownership this century, while the increase of owner-occupied houses to nearly 100 has had negligible impact on the pattern of landownership. Fig 10.3 shows at a local level the increase in owners before the mid 17th century and the subsequent re-concentration. The three main estates that became established at that time have also reflected the wider degree of continuity amongst landowning families. These three estates have been with the families of the present owners since the early 20th century, the mid 19th century and the late 16th century.

The different local patterns of landownership are the details that lie behind the statistics for Scotland as a whole. These local variations limit the value of any general description and, while one county has been used here to penetrate below the Scottish statistics, this inevitably creates a degree of bias in the wider perspective presented. However, the extent of diversity within Scotland's pattern of feudal landownership has always been limited. The degree to which the pattern has been dominated by the 1,500 largest estates has restricted the opportunity for anything but large-scale ownership.

'A Pattern of Landownership in Scotland' has provided an outline description of the evolution of that pattern. This information represents the first phase of a wider investigation into landownership in Scotland. The second phase has looked at 'The Power behind the Pattern'. This has involved examining the key factors that have determined the degree of continuity and change in the pattern of landownership and the influence of the pattern on the development of Scotland's rural communities and environment.

A few statistics that illustrate the relative constancy over so many centuries in both the structure of estates and their distribution within Scotland, might suggest a simple physical basis to this persistent

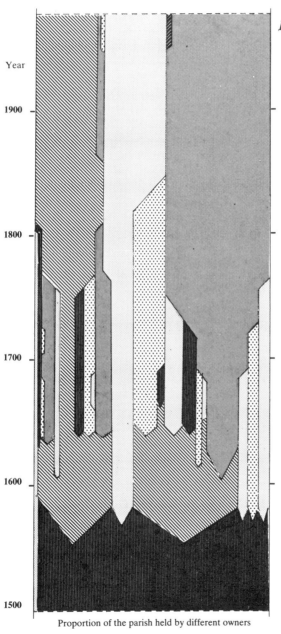

*Fig 10.3
Landownership in Birse
1500-1970*

The diagonal lines
represent the period in
which different properties
emerged or disappeared
as independently owned
units.

Year

1900 –

1800 –

1700 –

1600 –

1500 –

Proportion of the parish held by different owners

pattern. Mountainous areas and extensive tracts of low grade hill ground tend naturally to result in large-scale units of management and both these types of land are certainly widespread in Scotland. For example, 50% of Scotland's land area is above the conventional upland threshhold of 600 feet (182m.) and nearly 75% of Scotland's agricultural land (over 80% of the total land area) is classified as being limited in its productive potential to rough grazing.

Land quality has undoubtedly been an important basic influence on the pattern of landownership in Scotland and the present distribution of large estates does indeed broadly correlate with the areas of lower land quality. However, land quality by itself can not be used to explain, or to justify, the longstanding pattern of large-scale land-ownership in Scotland. Land quality has been only one of several key factors and even then, its influence has been through land values more than any necessary scales of management.

The increase in the number of landowners and the reduction in the extent of land held by the larger estates since the 19th century, when virtually all of rural Scotland was held within large estates, illustrate how the size of those estates was not just dependent on physical factors. Similarly, the gradual spread of these changes across the landscape shows simply that large estates have usually managed to survive longer on the less valuable land. An important reminder that compiling lists of estates based on their acreage does not coincide with the economic value or influence of these estates, as a few acres of prime arable land can be worth more than several hundred acres of hill ground.

Despite the decline during the last 100 years in the extent of Scotland's land held within large estates, Scotland still has a more concentrated pattern of private landownership than any other country in Europe. Indeed, initial research has failed to find a country anywhere with a pattern of private landownership that can match that found in Scotland. This pattern of landholdings is also only one measurement of landownership in Scotland. Within Scotland's ancient and complex feudal system, there is also the hidden pattern of superiorities. Superiors are, by definition, the disposers or sellers of land and while the number of landowners has increased during the last hundred years, the ownership of superiorities has not increased to the same degree. The pattern of landownership in Scotland as represented by the pattern of superiorities has remained much more concentrated than the pattern represented by the boundaries of landholdings on a map. The owners of estates that have contracted in size since the 19th century still typically retain the rights of superiority over the whole extent of the former estate lands.

The greater continuity in the pattern of superiorities than the pattern of landholdings reflects the fact that the relationship between Scotland's unique feudal system and Scotland's markedly concentrated pattern of landownership compared to other countries, is not one of chance. The ownership of land in Scotland has always granted landowners wide ranging rights over their land and the people living on it. These rights have conferred social, economic and political advantages on their holders and provided the basis of the power behind Scotland's persistent pattern of landownership. Scotland's landowners have always sought to maintain and strengthen their control over their land and their success can be indicated by the observation of Sir John Sinclair quoted in Chapter 9: 'In no country in Europe are the rights of proprietors so well defined and so carefully protected'.

The ways in which the rights of landowners over their land have changed during the long history of feudalism in Scotland, have involved two main trends. Firstly, the law has been developed to complete the landowners' monopoly over the resources on their land and secondly, the law has also been used to narrow the wide powers of earlier feudal property rights. The political influence of landowners has always limited these restrictions on their rights, but the history of sporting rights in Scotland can be used to illustrate these two directions of change.

There was no relationship between sport and landownership when feudalism became established in Scotland. Any free person could hunt any wild animal where they wanted and the game belonged to the person who killed or captured it, regardless of where they did this. However, over the centuries and culminating in an Act of 1621, sport was successfully converted into an exclusive right of property. As this could not be achieved by claiming ownership over the wild animals, it was established by making landowners the only ones who could hunt on their land. This is still the legal position today, although legislation since the 17th century has limited the nature of the landowners' exclusive right. Acts of parliament have steadily shortened the list of the species of wild animals which landowners can kill on their land, progressively reduced the choice of methods they can employ and the length of the hunting seasons available to them. At the same time, some species have survived outside the landowners' monopoly as 'vermin', while some rights over other species have been given to other people in special circumstances. For example, the Acts from the 1880s onwards allowing agricultural and crofting tenants to deal with rabbits, hares and deer that are causing serious damage to their crops.

Legislation that affects the rights of landowners continues to accumulate on many aspects of rural landuse and settlement. These statutes can be construed as an erosion of property rights to the extent that they regulate the powers of landowners over their land and the people living on it. However, by virtue of being restrictions, they have not tended to create opportunities outside the landowners' control. All the main rural resources including those for agriculture, forestry, sport, nature conservation, recreation, quarrying, settlement and development, remain controlled within the same pattern of landownership.

The power of landownership in Scotland has always meant that the pattern of landownership has had a profound influence on rural landuses and rural communities. The survival of Scotland's long-standing pattern of large-scale landownership reflects the continuing great importance of landownership's influence on rural Scotland. This makes landownership a central factor in any consideration of the future for rural Scotland, both to meet the aspirations of rural communities and of society at large for its rural environment. Landownership, covering the character and distribution of the rights over land and other natural resources, is a key variable that can be changed to break the spiral of decline in which rural Scotland has been locked for so long.

For nine centuries, feudal landownership has controlled the relationship between people and place in Scotland. The ideas and values of this ancient system, developed as legal theory and expressed as law, represent one way of governing this fundamental relationship. Modern ideas and values may require a different approach and this will involve re-writing the Law of the Land, so that it represents contemporary theories of an appropriate relationship between people and place.

Sources

This list mainly consists of the references from which specific information has been quoted in the text. Also included are the volumes in 'The New History of Scotland' series published by Edward Arnold, as these provide useful descriptions of the wider changes in Scotland during the period discussed in this book.

Adams, I. *The Division of Commonties in Scotland.* Ph.D. Thesis, Edinburgh University. 1967.

Adams, I. (ed.) *Directory of Former Scottish Commonties.* Scottish Record Society. 1971.

Armstrong, A. *Geographical Aspects of the Ownership, Management and Use of Rural Landed Estates in the Northern Highlands.* Ph.D. Thesis, University of Aberdeen. 1980.

Anon. *New Statistical Account of Scotland.* Blackwoods, Edinburgh. 1843.

Barrow, G. *Feudal Britain.* Edward Arnold, London. 1956.

Barrow, G. *Kingship and Unity, Scotland 1000-1306.* Edward Arnold, London. 1981.

Bateman, J. *Great Landowners of Great Britain and Ireland.* 4th Edn., Harrison, London. 1883.

Callander, R.F. *History in Birse.* (Vols I-IV). Callander, Finzean. 1981-5.

Callander, R.F. The Pattern of Landownership in Aberdeenshire in the 17th and 18th centuries. In: D. Stevenson (ed.) *'From Lairds to Louns'.* A.U.P., Aberdeen. 1986.

Callander, R.F. The Law of the Land. In: J. Hulbert (ed.) *'Land: Ownership and Use'.* Fletcher Society, Dundee. 1986.

Campbell, A. *The Grampians Desolate.* Edinburgh. 1804.

Carter, I. *Farm Life in North East Scotland 1840-1914.* John Donald, Edinburgh. 1979.

Carter, I. The Raid on Bennachie. Pages 119-125. In: A. Whiteley (ed.) *'Bennachie Again'*. Bailies of Bennachie. 1983.

Clark, G. *Some Secular Changes in Land-ownership in Scotland.* Pages 27-36. Scottish Geographical Magazine, 97(1). 1981.

Clark, G. *Public Ownership of Land in Scotland.* (Unpublished Ms. 1981.)

Conacher, H.M. *Land Tenure in 17th Century Scotland.* Pages 18-50. Judicial Review (50). 1938.

Dodgshon, R.A. *Land and Society in Early Scotland.* Clarendon Press, Oxford. 1981.

Grant, A. *Independence and Nationhood, Scotland 1306-1469.* Edward Arnold, London. 1984.

Grant, I. *Landlords and Land Management in North-east Scotland, 1750-1850.* Ph.D. Thesis, Edinburgh University. 1979.

Gilbert, J. *Hunting and Hunting Reserves in Medieval Scotland.* John Donald, Edinburgh. 1980.

Hamilton, H. (ed.) *Third Statistical Account of Scotland: The County of Aberdeen.* Collins, Glasgow. 1960.

Harrison, A. *et al. Landownership by Public and Semi-public Institutions in the U.K..* C.A.S., Reading. 1977.

H.M.S.O. *Owners of Lands and Heritages 1872-3 (Scotland).* House of Commons Accounts and Papers, 72(3). 1874.

H.M.S.O. *Report into the Acquisition and Occupancy of Agricultural Land.* Northfield Committee, Cmmd 7599. 1979.

H.M.S.O. *A Century of Agricultural Statistics 1866-1966.* 1968.

H.M.S.O. *Agricultural Statistics — Scotland.* (Annually).

Hunter Marshall, D.W. *Landholdings in 13th Century Scotland.* Unpublished. Ms. Gen. 1052, Glasgow University Library.

Huntly, Marquis of, *Records of Aboyne.* New Spalding Club, Aberdeen. 1894.

Johnston, T. *Our Scots Noble Families.* Forward, Glasgow. 1913.

Johnston, T. *The History of the Working Classes in Scotland.* Reprinted EP, Wakefield. 1974.

King, H. *Feudalism in Scotland.* Hodge, Edinburgh. 1914.

Knox, S. *The Scattalds of Shetland.* Ph.D. Thesis, Edinburgh University. 1980.

Mathers, A.S. *State-Aided Land Settlement in Scotland.* O'Dell Monograph No. 6, University of Aberdeen. 1978.

McEwen, J. *Who Owns Scotland.* EUSPB, Edinburgh, 1977.

McIntosh, J. *Historic Earls and Earldoms of Scotland.* Jolly, Aberdeen. 1898.

Michie, J. *Records of Invercauld.* New Spalding Club, Aberdeen. 1901.

Millman, R. *Maps of Scottish Estate Boundaries in 1970.* Scottish Record Office, (RHP 20,000).

Mitchison, R. *Lordship to Patronage, Scotland 1603-1745.* Edward Arnold, London. 1983.

Rankine, Sir J. *Laws of Landownership in Scotland.* Reprinted Green, Edinburgh. 1986.

Sanderson, M. *Scottish Rural Society in the 16th Century.* John Donald, Edinburgh. 1979.

Sinclair, Sir J. (ed.) *Statistical Account of Scotland.* Creech, Edinburgh. 1791-99.

Sinclair, Sir J. *General Report of the Agricultural State and Political Circumstances of Scotland.* Edinburgh. 1814.

Smith, A. (ed.) *A New History of Aberdeenshire.* Smith, Aberdeen. 1875.

Smith, Annette. *Jacobite Estates of the '45.* John Donald, Edinburgh. 1982.

Smout, T.C. *A History of the Scottish People, 1560-1830.* Collins, London. 1969.

Smyth, A.P. *Warlords and Holy Men, Scotland AD80-1000.* Edward Arnold, London. 1984.

Stevenson, D. *Alastair McColla and the Highland Problem in the 17th Century.* John Donald, Edinburgh. 1980.

Stuart, J. *List of Pollable Persons within the Shire of Aberdeen, 1696.* Spalding Club, Aberdeen. 1844.

Taylor, A. & J. (eds.) *Cess Roll for the County of Aberdeen, 1715.* Third Spalding Club, Aberdeen. 1932.

Taylor, A. & J. (eds.) *Valuation Roll of the County of Aberdeen, 1667.* Third Spalding Club, Aberdeen. 1933.

Timperley, L. *Landownership in Scotland in the 18th Century.* Ph.D. Thesis, Edinburgh University. 1977.

Timperley, L. *A Directory of Landownership in Scotland, c.1770.* Scottish Record Society. 1976.

Whyte, I. *Agriculture and Society in 17th Century Scotland.* John Donald, Edinburgh. 1979.

Wormald, J. *Court, Kirk and Community, Scotland 1470-1625.* Edward Arnold, London. 1891.

Appendices

Appendix A

Map of Aberdeenshire's Parishes

Key: see numbered list of parishes in Appendix B.

Appendix B

Heritors in Aberdeenshire 1667-1970

The numbers of 'heritors' in each Aberdeenshire parish by districts.

PARISH	AREA (acres)	1667	1696	1771	1791	1843	1872[1]	1970[2]
(DEESIDE)								
1. Kincardine O'Neil	18,182	17	12	11	12	11	15	16
2. Lumphanan	8,585	10	9	5	4	7	8	14
3. Coull	9,047	4	4	3	3	4	4	8
4. Tarland	6,300	8/5	6/6	5/4	7/6	8	10	1
5. Logie-Coldstone	13,977	3/5	4/5	7	4	5	5	10
6. Birse	31,591	21	15	7	6	4	4	4
7. Aboyne & Glen Tanar	24,891	10/7	6/6	3	3	3	3	10
8. Glenmuick, Tullich & Glen Gairn	87,335	7/12/9	5/11/8	8	7	4	7	6
9. Crathie & Braemar	182,219	17/13	10/9	8	8	3	3	6
(ALFORD)								
10. Alford	9,105	11	8	6	6	6	6	20
11. Leochel-Cushnie	12,858	4/4	3/4	5	5	5	5	8
12. Tough	7,109	9	6	7	6	4	5	9
13. Midmar	10,561	5	3	4	2	4	2	5
14. Cluny	10,045	6	5	8	2	5	4	7
15. Kemnay	5,113	2	2	2	2	3	4	5
16. Monymusk	10,728	2	1	1	1	1	2	1
17. Kcig	8,062	9	6	6	6	5	4	6
18. Tullynessle & Forbes	11,283	3/1	3/1	3	3	2	3	11
19. Auchindoir & Kearn	15,309	12/1	6/1	6	9	8	5	9
20. Kildrummy	10,349	4	5	3	4	4	3	4
21. Towie	16,736	7	8	5	4	5	5	6
22. Glenbuchat	11,089	2	2	1	1	1	1	2
23. Strathdon	53,681	16	17	10	5	7	6	7
TOTALS FOR DEESIDE & ALFORD DISTRICTS	574,155	246	197	128	116	109	114	175
Average Number of Heritors per Parish	(23 Parishes)	10.7	8.6	5.6	5.0	4.7	5.0	7.6
(HUNTLY)								
24. Huntly	12,476	6/5	1	2	2	2	7	16
25. Drumblade	9,318	5	6	4	4	5	6	25
26. Forgue	17,360	16	15	13	14	14	12	16
27. Cairnie	15,818	12	3	1	1	3	2	23
28. Glass	12,590	3	3	5	2	1	1	9
29. Gartly	18,038	5	1	2	1	1	2	24
30. Rhynie	12,875	8	2	2	1	1	1	9
31. Kennethmont	8,468	8	7	5	4	4	4	18
32. Clatt	5,715	7	7	2	2	2	2	7

Landownership in Scotland

PARISH	AREA (acres)	1667	1696	1771	1791	1843	1872[1]	1970[2]
(GARIOCH)								
33. Chapel of Garioch	13,060	21	13	17	10	12	10	(16)
34. Inverurie	4,948	8	7	7	7	5	6	9
35. Kintore	9,098	1	1	2	2	2	4	21
36. Keith-hall & Kinkell	7,599	7/5	3/5	2	2	3	3	6
37. Bourtie	5,692	8	6	4	5	5	4	24
38. Meldrum	8,104	3	2	2	1	1	8	10
39. Daviot	4,453	5	5	4	4	5	4	11
40. Rayne	7,886	17	11	5	5	6	8	9
41. Culsalmond	6,992	8	3	4	4	5	5	9
42. Insch	8,371	13	10	6	6	5	7	9
43. Oyne	10,131	14	9	3	3	4	7	16
44. Premnay	5,433	6	5	4	4	4	6	10
45. Leslie	4,446	3	3	2	4	2	2	9
TOTALS FOR HUNTLY & GARIOCH DISTRICTS	208,871	194	128	98	88	92	111	306
Average number of Heritors per Parish	(22 Parishes)	8.8	5.8	4.5	4.0	4.2	5.0	13.9
(TURRIFF)								
46. Turriff	18,404	27	13	9	6	12	12	27
47. King Edward	17,592	15	11	5	6	6	8	15
48. Monquhitter	17,435	10	10	7	11	12	12	18
49. Fyvie	29,584	21	11	10	8	8	9	33
50. Auchterless	16,834	16	9	5	6	2	8	26
(ELLON)								
51. Foveran	10,524	13	6	6	5	5	10	22
52. Slains	9,154	9	2	2	2	2	3	13
53. Cruden	18,237	4	4	5	5	10	13	18
54. Logie-Buchan	6,684	10	9	7	7	7	8	7
55. Ellon	23,137	15	12	6	6	8	11	22
56. Methlick	13,969	6	4	2	1	1	1	5
57. Tarves	16,301	14	6	2	2	2	1	9
58. Udny	11,242	14	7	11	11	8	15	19
(DEER)								
59. Peterhead	9,188	7	10	7	11	26	28	14
60. St Fergus	8,767	1	1	1	1	2	2	12
61. Crimond	7,240	8	7	4	4	4	3	11
62. Lonmay	11,238	5	7	5	5	7	9	15
63. Rathen	9,597	7	7	9	10	8	11	14
64. Fraserburgh	5,645	4	4	2	4	1	13	14
65. Pitsligo	4,646	4	4	4	5	3	4	8
66. Aberdour	14,033	4	4	2	2	2	2	8
67. Tyrie	11,184	5	5	5	5	4	3	8
68. Strichen	14,409	3	3	4	2	1	2	17
69. New Deer	26,754	24	19	11	11	9	10	31
70. Old Deer	27,372	—	—	9	11	9	1	24
71. Longside	16,844	13	7	6	6	8	7	23

PARISH	AREA (acres)	1667	1696	YEAR 1771	1791	1843	1872[1]	1970[2]
TOTALS FOR TURRIFF, ELLON & DEER DISTRICTS	375,951	259	182	146	153	167	206	435
Average number of Heritors per Parish	(26 Parishes)	10.0	7.0	5.6	5.9	6.4	7.9	16.7
(ABERDEEN)								
72. Belhelvie	12,155	6	6	7	16	15	14	11
73. Drumoak	7,239	1	1	3	3	4	5	3
74. Dyce	5,362	8	7	4	(5)	6	8	(12)
75. Echt	11,952	10	7	3	4	4	2	1
76. Fintray	7,270	7	6	5	5	4	5	12
77. Kinnellar	4,327	7	5	5	7	7	7	12
78. Newhills	8,685	9	4	4	(7)	10	28	(34)
79. New Machar	9,306	9	6	9	7	6	8	7
80. Old Machar	7,038	28	19	22	(26)	35	10	(12)
81. Peterculter	11,580	9	3	9	6	8	13	(12)
82. Skene	10,247	6	3	4	4	14	16	14
TOTALS FOR ABERDEEN DISTRICT	95,161	100	67	76	90	113	118	130
Average number of Heritors per Parish	(11 Parishes)	8.8	6.1	6.9	8.2	10.3	10.7	11.8
TOTALS FOR COUNTY	1,254,138	799	574	488	447	481	549	1,046
AVERAGE FOR COUNTY	(82 Parishes)	9.7	7.0	5.5	5.5	5.9	6.7	12.8

Notes:

1. These landowners held property in the parish assessed at £100 valuation; the heritors at earlier dates were simply those with heritable property in the parish.

2. These landowners owned 100 acres or more in the parish.

Appendix C

Some Records of Common Land in Aberdeenshire

There will have been areas of common land in each of the 82 parishes in Aberdeenshire. However, there is little information available on these areas at present. There are no records from 44 of the parishes and the records from most of the others are very limited.

The records for the parishes of Fraserburgh, Huntly, Inverurie, Old Machar and Peterhead were given in Chapter 8 under 'Burgh Commons'. An indication of the records for another 32 parishes is given in the first section here. The majority of these records come from Ian Adams' "Directory of Former Scottish Commonties" (Scottish Record Society, 1971). Ordnance Survey references are given in brackets.

There is no doubt that local research could increase these records. The second section here examines the Aberdeenshire parish of Birse to illustrate the range and extent of common lands that might be discovered within a single locality.

(i) Parish Records

Aboyne & Glen Tanar

Charters in 'The Records of Aboyne' (Spalding Club, 1894) imply more than one commonty near Aboyne but only the Commonty of Bellwood (NO 5498) is named. Many unspecific references also occur to common grazings, commonties, common woods and other shared rights in Glen Tanar. The Moss of Tilliehardie and the Black Moss, both near Auchinhove, were common and there were shared rights in the Lochs of Auchinhove and Auchlossan.

Auchindoir & Kearn

Correen Common Pasturage consisted of 415 acres of hill ground east of Glencairn farm towards Brux Hill (NJ 4921). It was the exclusive property of Lord Forbes, not a commonty, and was divided in 1875.

Clova estates received 50 acres and the Glebe of Auchindoir received two acres of the common in lieu of the privilege of pasture.

Belhelvie

562 acres of runrig land on Blairton (NJ 9117) were divided in 1768. The Muir of Drum Commonty was divided at the same time, but the Red Moss of Belhelvie remained in common between several proprietors. In 1840, a small area of undivided common was reported in the north-west corner of the parish.

Birse

— see section (ii) below.

Cairnie

A plan of 1766, showing the runrig lands of Haggieshall and Cormalet, describes the land south of Haggieshall (now the Bin Forest) as 'Good green pasture in common'.

Clatt

1,800 acres of the parish remained as undivided common in 1842.

Cluny

The Commonty of the Muir of Dalherrick was situated on low ground south of Tillycairn (NJ 6610) and reached into Midmar. A summons for division was raised in 1833.

Crathie & Braemar

There was no undivided land in 1842. 'The Records of Invercauld' (New Spalding Club, 1901) contain suggestions of several commonties in this parish, but no details.

Crimond

The Commonty of the Mosses of Crimongate (NJ 0458) was divided in 1779. The Commonty of the Mosses of Crimond (NK 0354) was divided after a summons in 1808. There was no undivided land in 1840.

Drumoak

The Commonty of the Hill or Muir of Coldstream and Keithmuir was divided in 1807. It extended to 216 acres and lay to the south-west of Drum Castle (NO 7899).

Echt

An early division of lands lying between the Kirkton of Echt (NJ 7305) and Tulleoch occurred in 1566. Early records also suggest other commonties in the same neighbourhood such as a commonty between Culquhousie and Dunecht Hill in 1585 (NJ 7407). The Hill of Fare Commonty, which was 7,700 acres and spread into Echt, was divided in 1707. In 1842 there was no undivided land.

Ellon

The Commonty of Mountforthie was divided in 1781. It lay north of Whitestone Hill (NJ 9739) and extended to 513 acres. A farm to the north-east of Ellon still bears the name Commonty (NJ 9632), but there is no other record of a commonty there.

Foveran

The Red Moss of Foveran covered 272 acres to the west of the Hill of South Fardine (NJ 9739). A summons was raised in 1868, but it was still undivided in 1871.

Gartly

The Commonty of Malsach Hill included the adjoining moorland. An action was raised for its division in 1844.

Glass

It was reported in 1842 that almost the whole of the highest hills were undivided common.

Glenmuick, Glengairn and Tullich

In 1842 there was no undivided land, but 'The Records of Aboyne' (Spalding Club, 1894) include many unspecific mentions of common woods, common rights and commonties in Glenmuick. The place name 'Cots on the Commonty' exists near Cambus O'May (NO 404980) and appears associated with a former commonty on Culblean. The Forest of Morven was subject to common rights.

Insch

Five acres of the Commonty of Insch remained undivided in 1842.

Kincardine O'Neil

The Commonty of the Hills of Dalhaikie and Beltie was divided in 1811 and 1814. The total extent is not known, but the second date refers to 36 acres that had escaped the first action (NO 6399).

Kintore

The Commonty of the Muir of Kintore was south of the Don and south-east of the Burgh (NJ 8013). A summons was raised in 1838.

Logie Coldstone

The inhabitants of this parish had common rights in the Forests of Morven and Culblean.

Lonmay

The Moss of Blairmormond near Dartfield (NK 0157) and of unknown extent, was divided in 1776.

Lumphanan

Stothill (NJ 5903) is referred to as a commonty in the Third Statistical Account, while common rights were held at Glenshalg (NJ 5906).

Midmar

Incorporated parts of the Commonties of Dalherrick (see Cluny) and Hill of Fare (see Echt).

Monymusk

The Commonty of the Hill of Tulloch (now Pitfichie Forest) extended to 3582 acres and appears to have been divided in 1799. The Commonty of Todlachie disappeared when the whole lands came into the possession of a single proprietor, Grant of Monymusk.

New Deer

Two farm names, Commonty and North Commonty (NJ 8648), suggest a former commonty in this location.

Oldmeldrum

In 1842 there was an undivided common of about 25 acres near Oldmeldrum.

Oyne

The Commonty of Bennachie covered 4,000 acres and was subject to legal disputes from at least 1738. Its eventual division in 1859 was ratified in 1889 following 40 years uninterrupted possession by the 9 estates that had shared in the division.

Pitsligo

The Commonty of Cairnhill was divided around 1811. For the Red Moss see Rosehearty in Burgh Commons, Chapter 8.

Rathen

The Commonty of the Hill of Mormond (NJ 9757) was divided in 1775. In 1840 there was no undivided land.

Strathdon

The Commonty of Breagach and Greenhill occupied the spur projecting northwards to the Water of Nochty (NJ 3215). It extended to over 600 acres and was divided in 1871. The Commonty of the Forest of Bunzeach was of considerable extent and was still undivided in 1855. The Commonty of Meikle Glenoughty spread from Peat Hill (NJ 2913) to the ridge of the Ladder Hills. It covered 3,134 acres and a summons for its division was raised in 1864.

Strichen

Incorporated part of Mormond Hill Commonty (see Rathen).

Tough

The Commonty of the Forest of Corrennie covered about 2,000 acres of the ridge between Tough, Cluny and Kincardine O'Neil parishes. It was divided in 1853. In 1842 it had been reported that 6,000-7,000 acres were in undivided common, but that 'what proportion of that tract belongs to the parish is hard to say'.

Tullynessle & Forbes

The Commonty of Balquharn was recorded in 1594 (NJ 5618).

(ii) The Common Lands of Birse

The parish of Birse, which has an area of 31,000 acres (12,550 ha), occupies the south-east corner of Aberdeenshire and is situated on the Highland:Lowland divide that cuts across the county.

Local research shows that all the main forms of common land have occurred in the parish: commonties, common mosses, runrig and common grazings, loans and greens, and a crown common.

Examples of common land still survive in Birse, most notably the Forest of Birse Commonty, which covers 9,000 acres (3,650 ha). The complex distribution of rights over the Forest illustrates many of the difficulties that can be encountered in trying to distinguish between common ownership and common use during historical research. The distinction was one that the Rev Joseph Smith, a Minister of Birse and a great authority on the parish, cautiously avoided when he recorded in 1790 that, "To the parish belong in property or at least by servitude, four forests or glens . . . Glen-Birse, Glen-Aven, Glenchatt and Glen-sleudrum".

However, the origins of the extensive rights of servitude in the parish were the same as those for the rights of common property. Both derived from patterns of feudal landownership super-imposed on patterns of traditional common use by the local inhabitants of the parish.

During the first five centuries of feudal landownership, the whole of Birse parish was a single unit, held first by the Crown and then by the Church. Traditional areas of common usage were therefore unaffected by property rights, except in as much as these landowners regulated the activities of their tenants.

This pattern continued until the 16th century when the Church lands were broken up and sold. By the mid 17th century there were over 20 separate properties or estates, with the local community fragmented between them. As a result of this, a complex mass of rights of servitudes and shared rights of property became established over areas of traditional common usage.

Records from that period show that those common rights covered approximately half the total land area of the parish. This figure is a minimum because of inadequate historical sources. However, it does match estimates that half Scotland was still common land in 1500.

During the increase in landowners in Birse, each estate originally derived their common rights, whether of property or servitude, from the distribution of their tenants' areas of traditional usage. However, by the 18th century, the emphasis had changed to determining the rights of tenants by the phrasing in each estate's title deeds.

Several areas of common land in Birse have been the subjects of legal contests and in some instances this resulted in their division between the competing landowners. However, many areas of common land simply disappeared due to a reconcentration of landownership.

The number of estates had fallen from over 20 to 4 by the 19th century. As a result, many rights of servitude and shared rights of property were re-absorbed into single units of ownership. Common use by that estate's tenants often still continued but changes in landuse and settlement were reducing these practises.

Figure C.1 maps areas in Birse that have been common land. An outline of each area's history is given in the Key that follows. More details on many of the areas can be found in 'History in Birse' Nos 1-4 (Callander, 1981-85).

Fig. C1   The Common Lands of Birse

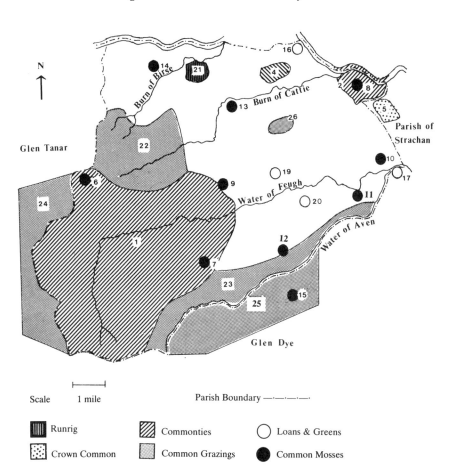

Key to Map of Common Lands in Birse

Commonties

1. *Forest of Birse:* Still covers about 9,000 acres (3,650 ha). Not strictly a commonty, as one Heritor in the parish owns the solum and only two Heritors share the sporting rights. All the other uses of the forest are still shared in common by the Heritors of Birse. A long history of disputes.

2. *Forest of Sleudrum:* Covered about 400 acres (162 ha) and was divided as a commonty in 1868 between two estates.

3. *Commonty Fishings:* On the Dee adjacent to the Forest of Sleudrum and survived 19th century legal disputes. It is still shared by the two estates that divided the Sleudrum Commonty.

4. *Commonty Wood:* A place name in Ballogie. No other definite information exists about this commonty, but it was centred on Craigmore Hill.

Crown Commons

5. *The Shooting Greens:* Unknown original extent, but it appears, like the Sleudrum Commonty, to have previously extended to the west of the Cairn o'Mount road. Taken over by the Crown Commissioners who granted rights over it to the Forestry Commission in 1930s, while two Birse estates subsequently gave up their rights in it. Legal confusion still exists (see 'Crown Commons'. Chapter 8).

Common Mosses

6,7,8. *Black Moss, Glaspits and Moss of Strathseven:* Histories as per commonties in which they occur. Many other sites in these commonties were also used for peat cutting.

9,10,11,12. *Mosses of Garbet, Rouen, Powlair and Luther Muir:* All came into the possession of a single estate by the late eighteenth century. They continued to be used in common by the tenants of several different farms, which had previously been separate small estates.

13,14. *Mosses of Birse and Ballogie:* There are indications that there were several mosses local to these two districts of the parish.

15. *Airy Muir:* Extensive area adjacent to Birse over which one estate in Birse still has rights of servitude, including peat cutting and grazing. (See No. 26).

Loans and Greens

16,17. *Potarch, Whitestones:* Two small stances associated with river crossings of the Cairn o'Mount road. They still remain as commons. (See 'Greens'. Chapter 8).

18. *Cairn o'Mount, Fungle:* Two ancient route ways which provide important north-south passes across the Mounth. The former in the east of the parish continues as a public road, while the latter in the west of the parish has had to be contested even to maintain it as a right of way.

19,20. *Turfgate, Foggie Loan:* Two place names which both indicate shared routes to common lands.

Rights of Way

These were not common property, but an extensive local network existed connecting the various commons and other public places. Many are lapsing either through disuse or obstruction. No attempt has been made to mark them on Fig C.1.

Runrig and Common Grazings

21. *Kinminity:* Involved about 100 acres (40 ha) of cultivated ground as runrig land and about 500 acres (200 ha) of common hill, and survived into the 19th century because part was owned by the Kirk Session. The largest Heritor in the parish, who already owned three quarters of the rigs, persuaded the Kirk Session to sell him their Quarter of Kinminity rather than to go to court for a division.

Common Grazings & Sheilings

22. *Glencat:* Traditionally used in common by tenants of several estates, but the rights were interpreted as being servitudes, as 17th century title deeds specified a share (e.g. one fifth of . . .). Sporting rights are still however shared between two heritors.

23. *Glen Aven:* Like Glencat, an extensive area traditionally associated as a common with the Forest of Birse, but was also separated off like Glencat in the 17th century. In the 18th century all the properties sharing the use of the area came into the possession of one estate, except for a small area at the head of Glen Aven. This is still shared in property between two estates.

24. *Glen Tanar:* Tenants in part of Birse had extensive rights at the head of this adjoining Glen until the early 19th century. They

disappeared when the lands in Birse and Glen Tanar became the property of a single proprietor.

25. *Glen Dye:* One estate in Birse has servitudes, including peat and grazing rights which were last legally contested in the 1930s, over an extensive area from the River Aven to its southern skyline, thus incorporating the bulk of Mount Battock.

26. *Midstrath:* Previously a separate estate in Birse, over which another estate held servitudes. However, the servitudes were resigned in 1868 in exchange for 55 acres (22 ha) in outright ownership.